PAST & PRESENT TENSE

PAST & PRESENT TENSE

A Northern boy's journey through life
London and the swinging 60's

STEWART RUSSELL BURNETT

Printed by Kindle Direct in the United Kingdom

First Printing, June 2019

This book is written primarily for the benefit of my four children, but if anyone else feels like reading it, you are welcome. I hope you find it of interest.

Thanks are due to all my children for the pleasure they have (not always) brought me, but to Cosima, my special thanks for acting as my 'Editor'. She exterminated countless commas and saved me from several of my potentially embarrassing and politically incorrect remarks. It took her time and effort, and I am grateful.

CONTENTS

Past Tense

Pudsey

I think the very first memory I can recall, is of four smiling female faces looking reassuringly, lovingly down at me. Perhaps they were trying—at least in part—to reassure themselves. This scene, lit only by candlelight, was set in the Anderson air raid shelter the men of the family had dug, deep into the back garden of our council house. It was nineteen forty-five, and I was three years old.

It has been suggested that this is not a memory at all, but just an idea put in my head by family, later in life. However, the image of those smiling faces—my mother (Annie) and three sisters, Marie, May and Sylvia, illuminated against the darkness of the shelter, is vivid and I choose to believe it real. Another memory is being woken late at night and brought downstairs, to discover my brother Eddie had returned from the war. The whole family sat around the dining table, piled high with the contents of his army issue kitbag—tinned peaches, pears, salted butter and condensed milk, among a seemingly endless variety of things. For me, he had a Dinky-Toy, eight-wheeled-petrol tanker. I sat on his knee listening to the adult chatter and playing with my shiny new toy. Over the following days and weeks, he would tell me many stories about his army service.

One such story was when he was stationed in Palestine and performing guard duties at an internment camp. The camp was holding the Jewish refugees from Europe, who were trying to get into Israel. A detainee was holding a camp official hostage and threatening his life. One of the guards shot him between the eyes, over the hostages head.

The war was now over and life could only get better. There were Street parties held everywhere. Rationing, however, continued—even so, I remember my amazement and pleasure, when eating my first banana.

Nineteen forty-seven brought the dreadful winter, but we children—of course—managed to capitalise on this. The housing estate was on the side of a steep hill and was consequently—sledging paradise.

As the local delivery lorries couldn't get through, my sister Sylvia and I were periodically tasked with collecting a sack of coal, from the local depot and bringing it home on my sledge. Nothing mechanised could get through.

The snow was so thick; we had to tunnel out of the house. Eventually, when the snow melted, we were left with a thick slab of ice on the estate roads. All the neighbours came out 'en masse', with picks and shovels to remove the ice, thus allowing the estate to be reached by the local suppliers again. This was all exciting to me, and as the post-war community spirit was still so strong, it was exciting for everyone.

We lived at 72, Waterloo Grove, on a relatively new council house estate, just off Waterloo Road, Pudsey Yorkshire, England, the World. To my parents and older siblings, this was a very nice state of affairs; mum would tell stories of the previous houses they had lived in—squalid, cockroach infested, without basic amenities or even hot water. Terrifying images to me at the time, and even now, having encountered cockroaches myself in Greece and other hot countries, they are still scary. Every year—during my second marriage—on visiting our holiday home in Greece, we would enter the property with apprehension, wondering how many dead or living nasty creatures we would find.

These stories would be told to me on the days I was off school sick with cold or flu, and they always fascinated me, especially hearing about older family and relatives. Being the baby of the family—*the forty year 'surprise package'*—I never knew any of my grandparents or other relatives of that generation. We would be sat each side of the old black-leaded iron fireplace. It had an oven to one side and a hob on the other. the mantle shelf was higher than me. I remember the days she was baking bread or (on festive occasions) cake mix. The dough mix would be 'rising' in a large bowl on the floor, in front of the fire. Lovely smells.

There were stories of past possessions, properties and affluence, which had somehow been lost; I never did get to the bottom of these.

With the end of the war, things gradually got better, both socially and economically. The family was able to take annual holidays in Blackpool. These were communal group affairs, with singing and drinking on the hired coach journey. Approaching Blackpool, all the children would be straining to be the first to catch a glimpse of the sea—I think there was a few pence reward for the winner.

I found it an unworldly experience the first time we walked down the street from our bed & breakfast lodgings, seeing at the end of the street . . . nothing. Just emptiness. It was only on approaching closer to the raised promenade, that the sea became visible. Encountering the sea for the first time was completely overwhelming for me.

There were other trips to Blackpool, when all the delights were enjoyed—the trams, the illuminations and Pleasure Beach. I remember standing with a crowd of people around a large display case, containing the 'Laughing Policemen'. It was totally infectious—no one could resist laughing along with this crazy, swaying, police-automaton, accompanied by a recording of (slightly insane) laughter. The illuminations, the tower, the tower ballroom and circus, and the one and only Reginald Dixon, rising out of the ground playing the Wurlitzer organ,

"Oh, I do like to be beside the seaside,
I do like to be beside the sea,
I do like to stroll along the Prom, Prom, Prom,
Where the brass bands play,
Tiddely-om-pom-pom.
So just let me be beside the seaside!
I'll be beside myself with glee
And there's lots of girls beside
I should like to be beside,
Beside the seaside,
Beside the sea!"

Being shortly after the war, one of the most popular arcade games and surely a forerunner of today's many shoot-'em-up computer games was based on wartime film footage taken from the viewpoint of the mid-turret gunner on a Lancaster bomber. The film was Black & White and back-projected onto a screen, and there was a movable gun sight which you could control by a handle on the machine front. Grainy, Messerschmitt 109s attacked between the Lancaster's twin tails and

5

you had to shoot as many as you could. It was probably just a short piece of film, on a constant loop, but it was effective then and thrilled me to bits. The machine emitted a machine gun sound effect—'tum-tum-tum-tum-tum' and this was heard everywhere you walked on the promenade. It cost three pence a go. Inevitably, my parents grew weary of my constant requests for more threpnee bits. The 'What the Butler Saw' machines were quite interesting too—but not when my parents were supervising me. Sometimes Dad would take me for an early morning walk, while mum was still in bed. We would go to one of the seafront cafes and I would have a cup of tea while dad talked to other men in the café. They would ask questions which made me squirm in my seat. I can't really think of any other activities that took place one-on-one, with Dad. My memories tend to be all of interactions with my Mum. Other holidays were to Whitby, Scarborough and Bridlington on the East coast. From Whitby, we once took an outing on a beautiful old paddle steamer to Robin Hoods Bay—I spent most of the trip looking down into the engine room, watching the slightly scary, hissing and clanking beam engine.

The best holiday I had with my parents was to Butlins holiday camp in Filey. It was like being transported into a magical land, full of attractive men and women, wearing red blazers, white trousers and skirts.

Past Tense

It all seemed so glamorous and exciting then. A completely new world—especially for my parents, after the gloom, misery and despair of the war years. It was run like the schoolhouse system I would encounter, later in my education. Divided into groups and allocated our personal Redcoat, we competed against the other groups, in a great variety of bizarre ways—bathing belle pageants, knobbly knees contests, and prizes for the loudest snorer, shiniest bald head, bonniest Baby and most glamorous grandmother, etc. Meal times were communal (in a large dining hall) and were great fun, with the redcoats cavorting around entertaining their particular house group.

It was new and exciting for me in another way; I was allowed to roam freely within the—supposedly child safe—environment.

The Butlins concept was brilliant for families like mine, so soon after the war, but I would rather die than visit one now. Likewise, I would rather die than go on a cruise ship.

Number 72 was the house where I was born and raised, until I left college at nineteen and came to London. My unknown sister Audrey and my father both died in this house. The whole estate is now demolished and replaced with what Pete Seeger referred to in his popular song as "Little boxes, little boxes, little boxes made out of ticky-tacky. "

Clearly, the address tells you we were a working-class

family. I have encountered many professionals during my working life in London, who claimed to be working class—but no, not so. My father had no trade as such and I recall his entry once on some official document as 'Store Keeper' for the local English Electric factory. Like my brother Eddie and brother-in-law Des, he also worked for years at the David Brown factory.

As well as tractors, David Brown produced the Aston Martin and Lagonda cars. Every Christmas there would be a party for the workers and their families and we children received precious models of the cars from *'Santa Claus'*. To this day, I still feel a strong connection with, and admiration for, these beautiful cars—James Bond had excellent taste. Unfortunately, manufacturing was relocated and Dad ended up doing night shifts, stoking the furnace at the now mothballed works. The heat and coke dust was bad for his chest and took its toll on him in later life—perhaps contributing to his eventual death from bronchial problems.

A short distance from my home was a small petrol station. It was just a couple of the old upright petrol pumps, with the illuminated sign on top. Passing one day, I was overwhelmed to see a Mercedes-Benz 300 SL parked at the garage. It was just sitting there with both Gull-wing doors open to the sky. So futuristic, it was like a spaceship to me.

Marie and May worked in Waterloo Mill, just at the bottom of our road and I visited them one day to watch them working at the weaving looms. They were dressed in Green overalls and headscarves. The noise of the looms, with the brass, tipped, hardwood shuttles, as they flew from side to side was terrific, and even a little frightening to me. More frightening though was when my pet rabbit died, and with a friend I took it to the mill boiler room furnace. The two 'stokers' opened the furnace door and invited me to throw it in. The heat was so terrific I couldn't bear it, so my friend James Nailer stepped forward and did the deed. As his name suggests, he was a toughie, not one with whom to pick a fight. Even so, we did have fights from time to time. On one occasion, he had been making disparaging remarks about Dianna, a girl I liked. She wasn't the prettiest girl on the block, but she was a girl none the less. These fights never resulted in blows being landed or blood drawn—it was always pretend fighting, with care taken not to actually make contact. A bit like wild animals defending their territory, but not wanting to receive any life-threatening injuries.

The weapon of choice was our school caps, which were held so that the hard peak could cause pain, should it actually ever make contact. Of course, there would be endless wrestling matches when out in the local fields. One of the gang had a bow and arrows and he thought it was a great idea to shoot an arrow, straight up in the air while another idiot was wrestling with me to the ground. I struggled desperately to get free while the arrow was in the air for what seemed like an eternity. I just knew it was going to hit me on its return to earth, resulting in my premature death. The idiot wrestling me seemed unaware of the danger and I could not get free. When the arrow finally did return from the heavens, it pierced one of the wellington boots I was wearing, amazingly passing harmlessly between two toes — the boot was no longer waterproof and my big toe was sore for a couple of days.

My mother was clearly not well educated. Working class women of her generation were not generally encouraged to concern themselves with such matters — they were to keep house and bear children. As I grew older, I realised I'd never witnessed my mother writing anything down. My father (Norman) wrote the greeting cards or filled in any official forms. True, she did tick the boxes on the 'Littlewoods' football coupons — but that's not writing.

Looking back now, I realise it's quite possible she could not actually write. I will never know. But she did have a seemingly endless supply of 'Sayings' —

"An apple is gold in the morning, silver in the afternoon and lead at night."

and,

"An hour before midnight is worth all the hours after. "

If she caught me sighing – which I did a lot, she would say,

"Every time you sigh, you lose a drop of blood."

Some of these are quite wise and I still (sometimes), pay homage to them—certainly, I never eat an apple late at night. In my experience, think the hour before midnight also makes sense.

Dad was clearly more educated and sophisticated. Although I never saw him reading a novel, he appreciated (among other things), classical music. When I was a young child, he was a slightly scary figure of authority, but I don't recall him ever physically punishing me— whereas my mother certainly did. I remember once, scrambling frantically under the dining table, trying to escape the slaps on my bare legs—still wearing short trousers. I can't remember what I'd done to warrant this, but I almost certainly deserved it. Nevertheless, she was a loving mother to me. She used to cook nice meals (especially at weekends), and usually with fresh ingredients from the back garden. As a result of the war and rationing, everyone grew as much food as they could and every garden would be filled with vegetables—certainly not flowers. Weekday meals could be more basic—corned beef, jam or treacle sandwiches. I used to sneak into the pantry and take huge spoonfuls of malt extract from a jar, located on a high shelf— delicious. Mum used to make wonderful creamed rice pudding, which I could never get enough of. She would make a huge portion so there would be some left for the next day. This would set solid and you had to carve out chunks with a spoon. I absolutely preferred it this way. Again, I would sneak illicit spoonfuls, from the pantry. Rhubarb pudding was a regular treat—we had a huge patch of it in the garden. It was so tall, my friends and I used hide under the large leaves. It was one of my various chores to cut it and chop it into chunks, ready for cooking. Rhubarb crumble is still a favourite of mine.

After his return, Eddie and I had to share a bed, in one of the back bedrooms—there were three, but my parents and Sylvia had the other two.

One night when he was asleep, in the candlelight I could see an earwig coming out of his ear—I was horrified. I hated earwigs and moths; every night before getting into bed, I would go around the bedroom killing the moths with a rolled up newspaper. The earwigs originated from a refuse sack, my parents left hanging on the back garden fence—if you disturbed the sack, hundreds of them would pour out—terrifying. Eventually, Eddie met Jean, married her, and moved out of the family home. I'm sorry to say, the moths and earwigs remained. It took some time, but I finally managed to persuade my parents to remove the sack. Bedtimes became less of a 'Trial by the insect World'.

As young children, living on the doorstep of open

country, my friends and I were allowed to wander freely around. Paedophiles were not an issue then—the word probably didn't exist in the local vocabulary. Certainly, later in life, my four children were never allowed the same level of freedom.

Like us, our dog Trixie was also allowed complete freedom to roam. I don't recollect any family member ever taking Trixie for a walk. She just took herself off whenever she felt like it, and likewise returned. No litter trays, poop scoops or bags, in those days. Doors were left unlocked during the day and ritualistically, locked at night, before retiring to bed.

At times, we children were almost certainly a bit naughty. We always had some 'den' we would hide away in, and get up to childish mischief—doctors and nurses,

"show me yours and I'll show you mine."
the usual stuff that children probably still get up to—but then, probably not. That innocence and lack of knowledge no longer exists today. I seem to remember something about trying to insert pieces of straw into penises . . . all completely innocent.

One hot summer day, across the road, in a neighbours back garden, the den consisted of blankets over clotheshorse. I was in the den with Margaret Barker and we (somehow), both ended up naked. There were older girls in the garden with us and when a gust of wind dislodged one of the blankets, great screams went up,

"Look, they're both starkers!"

There was a lot of laughter too and no harm done. We were quickly returned to a fully clothed state.

We didn't know about sex or even understand why girls were different to boys, but it was a fascinating subject, that we never grew tired of researching. It wouldn't be until much later, that I would discover the 'Sex' subject and its purpose in life.

While Dianna and I certainly fooled around a lot, we had absolutely no inkling of what we were doing. One day we were playing in her back garden. We were lying in a sort of enclosure we had built from bits of junk and were on our sides, pressing ourselves closely together and perhaps there was some fumbling around—can't remember exactly. To my dismay, on looking up I saw her mother looking through the rear bedroom window. I don't know what she saw, or thought she saw, but nothing happened. We just froze and pretended that we weren't really doing anything naughty at all.

When I got sick with a badly swollen throat, the ambulance came, and as the medics carried me down the stairs, mum was crying bitterly—I didn't realise why at the time.

"What's wrong mum, what's wrong? "

I was in an isolation ward for two weeks, receiving painful injections in my behind.

Past Tense

After this, at home, sitting by the fire, mum explained there had been a fourth sister—Audrey. She had died at five years old from Diphtheria, seven years before I appeared on the scene. What I'd had was a severe bout of Tonsillitis—apparently the symptoms are very similar, and she was afraid I might die too. Many children died of Diphtheria; it was the third leading cause of child death in England during the 1930s. Audrey had the same birthday as Princess Margaret and whenever the Royal Birthday was announced in the media, I would be reminded of the sister I never knew. Many years later, attending a function at the London Design Centre, I was briefly introduced to the designer/photographer, Anthony Armstrong-Jones and his wife at the time—Princess Margaret. After due consideration, I decided it was best not to mention Audrey. The whole area and surrounding countryside was unusually hilly, providing us children with many opportunities for exploration and exciting activities—steep hills to slide down, Black Carr woods, disused quarries, old mill ponds, rivers, tunnels through huge railway embankments, abandoned coal mines, slag heaps, and Annie Jones resided just down the 'Jib' (Gibraltar Road), more dirt track than road.

She kept pigs, poultry and had a typical farm type shop—stone flag floors and all the produce in large open wooden bins. After a hard day's fun and games in the 'wilderness', a group of us might stop at Annie's on the way home, and ask for a drink of water. She never refused and when she went into the back room, we would help ourselves to a carrot each. I am sure she knew. I think she was related to my family in some vague, distant way. I still love raw carrots. I found her pigs fascinating, but slightly scary and disgusting—wallowing in their own shit. By contrast, the pigs at the Annual Pudsey Fair were always well groomed.

The fair was a great day out for all, with show jumping, army gun carriage racing, police motorcycle riding displays, and prizes for just about every farm animal you could think of—I particularly loved the enormous shire horses. The highlight of the day for us was at the end of the show when they started putting—or at least trying to put—all the livestock back onto the lorries. The pigs—huge great prize pigs—would create squealing mayhem, refusing to leave their temporary pens. When they did, they would go anywhere, except into the lorries.

In my early years, I was afraid of loud bangs—fireworks. On 'Guy Fawkes' (Plot), night, I would cower on the bathroom floor, with Trixie—both of us whimpering in unison. The arrangement was the *'grown-ups'* would let off all the explosive fireworks and then I could emerge and join in the fun with the pretty, quieter, fireworks. Poor Trixie chose to remain indoors for the duration. It was said this fear, was because I was a 'War-Baby', but this theory is unproven, and anyway,

Past Tense

I eventually lost my fear of loud bangs. In fact, plot night became an event my friends and I all looked forward to each year. There was much competition between 'gangs', to build the biggest bonfire. We would go off into the countryside and come back dragging small trees behind us. It was all serious stuff to us, and we felt important doing it.

The two or three weeks before plot night were almost more fun than the actual night. One year, we had this huge bonfire prepared. We had created a 'Den' in the hollow centre and this was our Fiefdom. We spent as much time as possible in there, only venturing out, to let off fireworks. It was a shame we had to burn it down. The night before Bonfire Night was 'Mischief Night', and we would play pranks: knock-and-run on neighbour's front doors, letting down car tyres, tying metal dustbin lids to doorknockers. It was the night we would try to pilfer wood from rival gang's bonfires, but they were usually well guarded.

On the actual night, after the bonfire had burnt down, parents would cook sausages and jacket potatoes, in the red-hot embers. My love of jacket potatoes originates there.

I always enjoyed making things, model boats, planes and toys; I was just as interested in blowing them up, especially around Guy Fawkes bonfire night. Inserting 'bangers' into damaged or unwanted models was great fun. My friends and I would also have competitions to see who could get an empty bean can to jump the highest. There weren't any expensive toys around my house, so making my own out of cardboard and balsa wood and then eventually blowing them up, was a great form of amusement. I was also just as—perhaps even more—interested in drawing and painting; consequently, Birthday and Christmas presents would often be a sketchpad and a box of watercolours. My late sister Marie was also a keen watercolourist, and I was surely influenced and encouraged by her.

A great source of model making material was 'Mabel Turnpenny'—the haberdashery shop at the bottom of our road. Empty shoe boxes, used bobbins and spare thread etc., were invaluable to me.

For the sake of honesty, I admit here that a friend and I once stole from Mabel Turnpenny. It was some tiny, meaningless thing, of no use or value to us—it was just the thrill of stealing something. As soon as the deed was done, we threw it away into a field. Somehow, we were lumbered—maybe Mabel saw us doing it. We were paraded in front of her by the local bobby and instructed to apologise—never stole again.

Another source of material was one of the local, disused stone quarries. For a long time, it used to be an exciting playground for us, clambering around the rock faces and the remains of heavy equipment, but then the Council started using it as a land-fill-site. Even then, it remained a source of interest and exploration. One Christmas, I received a basic Meccano starter kit. There wasn't a great deal you could make with it, but to my great joy, on one of my visits to the steaming, burning, foul-smelling land-fill, I found a huge quantity of Meccano components—cleaned and repainted, they allowed me to make all manner of elaborate constructions.

After plot night came Christmas—even better. My fondest memory, is Dad taking down the artificial tree and boxes of decorations from the cupboard above their wardrobe. The decorations were wrapped each year in the same old pages from newspapers, magazine and comics—Eagle, Dandy, Beano, Hotspur, Lion et al. I was always allocated the task of unwrapping them—and I would spend the whole time reading the comic pages—while my parents did the actual tree decoration. The tree was from Woolworths, had folding branches that looked like pipe cleaners, and lasted throughout my childhood. It was small and was located on top of the side table containing the large valve radio. The living-room would then be festooned with folding paper garlands, stretching from wall to wall above our heads. Lots of balloons of course, but blowing them up I was scared they would burst in my face—did not like loud bangs.

Getting to sleep on Christmas Eve was a challenge. But eventually, morning would come and I would wake to find a Christmas stocking hanging from the bed foot frame. It usually contained various edible treats and other minor items. More important, was the large pillow-case hanging there—stuffed with the *real presents*. Such delightful memories.

I always wanted to have roller skates, but I never did get any, I don't know why. I think they were too expensive for my parents. I did eventually get a bike though. A very basic thing at first, but I was gradually able to add things, like gears and lights. I was forever stripping it down into pieces and reassembling. It changed colour more than once.

We kids were always making catapults. This involved a trip into the woods, to find a suitable 'Y' shaped tree branch. We then cut strips from an old bicycle, inner-tube and made the pouch from a scrap piece of leather—I must say, a great deal of craftsmanship was involved in making these devices. We used them for all kinds of mischief, shooting tin cans and bottles—and (I'm sorry to say) birds.

It's hard to look back and realise how cruel children could be, without thinking anything of it. It was the countryside, and we were all a bit feral. If I managed to kill a bird, I would give it a ceremonial burial, under a nice tree, and place a little cross on the grave.

By the time I was old enough to have an air rifle, I had realised it wasn't nice to shoot birds—but then I did shoot a big, fat Woodpigeon once—I took it home, plucked it, my mother cooked it, and I ate it.

I then became a keen bird watcher, keeping a record of all the birds I observed—I was never without my copy of 'The Observer's Book of British Birds.' One of my favourite birds was the Kingfisher and one day, I actually managed to witness one in the act of catching a fish in a small brook. Birds of prey—Sparrow Hawks and Kestrels—were the ultimate birds to see. Even today, I find them beautiful and exciting. Especially Golden Eagles—never managed to see one of those.

Lapwings and Skylarks were also wonderful to watch and hear singing. To this day, whenever I hear the classical piece 'The Lark Ascending' by Vaughan Williams, I am transported back to a particular still, summer day spent out in the local countryside. I was strolling through a grassy meadow, when a Skylark rose suddenly from the grass some distance ahead of me and began hovering overhead singing its heart out—they lay their eggs on the ground, hidden in grass, and when anyone or anything approaches the nest, they try to distract attention and draw them away from the nest's location.

They swoop low and rise again to hover at height, constantly singing. I could not resist the challenge to find the nest, and after much patient searching, it was found, containing several eggs. I left the nest in peace, moving some distance away, from where I observed the lark descend back to the nest.

Pudsey

I also used to collect bird's eggs—not so good, I know, but I tried to do it responsibly. I would only take an egg if the nest contained several, and one would (hopefully), not be missed or cause distress. I had exotic eggs I could not have sourced myself—Ostrich, for example, provided by adults and obtained from where I know not.

My sister May was married to Des and my sister Marie was also married to Des—a different one. This one was a cockney immigrant in Yorkshire, whose skill lay in the art of riding motorbikes and driving trucks, both of which he did during the war in Germany.

May's Des was from a strong Catholic family—this fact caused varying degrees of friction between my Church of England family and his. He was a cut above us lot and went on to be a 'Professional'—a successful electrical engineering consultant. I never felt any real affection for him, whereas Marie's Des and I became close—both when I was a child and later in life. I would ride on the pillion of his 'Matchless' motorbike and help him strip down and rebuild the engine. He always seemed to be working on some motorbike engine so—as well as having a lot of fun—I gained a great deal of practical knowledge and mechanical skill.

Eventually, he progressed from motorbikes to cars. Yet more useful knowledge for me in later life. There were so few cars around in those days. For many years, there was just one car—a Ford Popular 103E, parked on Waterloo Grove. This left the streets completely free as playgrounds for us children.

For a little while he had an 'Allard J2' with the 3.6 L flathead V8 engine, from the Ford Pilot. This car was amazing, with a bonnet that seemed to go on forever. Once on a piece of derelict land, he let me drive it for a brief moment—it took off like a rocket and scared me to death, before Des heaved on the hand break.

Des told me many stories of his time in Germany, many of which concerned the sexual exploitation of the local female populace. It seems a bar of chocolate could get you almost anything. There were many stories which cannot be retold here—one such story involved a donkey . . . These stories should not have been told to a child my age—but I was fascinated and horrified at the same time.

At heart, he was like a child, happy to spend time with another child—he never seemed to have any adult friends, at least not that I was aware. As well as fooling around with motorbike and car engines, we spent countless hours playing with air rifles and pistols—constantly trying to make them more powerful by messing with the internal spring system. I made 'tracer' and 'explosive' slugs, by packing them with matchstick-head shavings and then sealing them with either Vaseline (for tracer), or aircraft model dope (for explosive). After dark, It was great fun, firing these at neighbour's chimney stacks—seeing the flash and hearing the crack.

Mary and Des never had any children and I don't know whether it was by choice, or if there was some medical reason. Des once said to me his work colleagues sometimes asked how he avoided children, to which he would reply,

"I keep an old sock by the side of the bed."

Whatever the reason, looking back now I think perhaps he thought of me as a substitute son. We certainly spent a lot of time together and he was probably more of a hands on father than my Dad was. I certainly enjoyed being with him as often as I could, and he didn't seem to mind my companionship. I remember the trips I sometimes took with him, in lorries delivering coke to the various factory boiler houses, around the north. This usually meant a very early morning start. On one such trip he was having a race with another lorry from his company, driven by a friend. Des' lorry had a diesel engine, which was stronger and faster up the long hills. The other was petrol driven and so faster on the downhill stretches. It went on for ages, constantly swapping the lead—much to my excitement. I learnt a lot about driving on main roads and manoeuvring around large vehicles. I think these lessons helped a lot when I learnt to drive, many years later.

I roamed freely around the streets and countryside

with the air rifle on a sling, over my shoulder. Des also loaned me an antique rifle, which I also paraded around the streets with. If one were to do this in the present day, there would be panic and armed police everywhere.

I once took my air-pistol to school, and during break time, my friends and I took pot shots at the windows of a derelict building, that was visible over the high, school wall. I do not know how we got away with this kind of behaviour—you certainly couldn't now.

Later, when I had departed for London, Des acquired a shotgun. On one of my visits to see mum and dad, I went out into Black Carr woods with him and the shotgun. His fiddling had not stopped—he was forever messing with the cartridges, trying to change their behaviour. As a child, I was full of admiration for him, but in later life, I came to realise how much his childish and—at times—quite selfish behaviour, affected my sister Marie. I remember him once using what little money spare money there was, to buy a bigger, better air rifle. Marie was upset, as she had plans for that money. I (of course), was on Des' side—we boys wanted our fun. It was events like this that much later caused me to feel regret and shame for my behaviour.

My early days at the local nursery school—were fun—but marred by the fact we had to have afternoon naps on camp beds. There was a coal-fired stove in the middle of the classroom—nice and cosy, but the trouble was, on being awakened, we were required to fasten our own shoelaces—this was a task completely beyond me. It seemed to me, life as a child was filled with such (with hindsight minor, but then major) personal humiliations. Then, there was the nightmare of my first day at primary school. Mum took me there and—for some reason beyond me—we arrived in the middle of a PE lesson in the main assembly hall. There seemed to be children as far as the eye could see. They were all sitting on oval shaped rush mats on the floor and gently rocking back and forth. Mum tried to hand me over to the tutor, but I yelled like hell and clung to her, refusing to let go.

Eventually, mum extricated herself from my clutches, and I was instructed to take a rush mat and join the other children. I hugged the mat around me as tightly as possible, rocking back and forth, until I regained my equilibrium. Thankfully, the children present didn't laugh, or mocked my humiliation—perhaps they all remembered their own. Maybe they were afraid of the tutor's wrath.

Physical punishment was the norm in schools then—I myself was caned on more than one occasion. One teacher had a 12" wooden ruler (with no markings) he called 'Brown Bess'. His routine was to give you a rap across your knuckles, as your hand was laid on your desk. I remember my friend, James during an

Past Tense

English lesson; he was stood in front of the teacher, and the whole class, trying hard to sound the 'h' in 'when.' The teacher eventually said,

"Blow, blow, blow."

at which he puffed out his cheeks and blew directly into her face—he was duly clattered around his head with the book she was holding. This was much to the amusement of the class. Nearing the end of the English lesson, this particular teacher would stage a little spelling competition—she would call out a word and you could put your hand up and try to spell it. If spelt correctly, the reward was, you got to leave the class early. It may have only been five minutes or so, but the feeling of achievement and superiority over your unfortunate classmates, who had to remain *another five minutes,* was immense. I was nearly home by then. Another strange memory from this school—whenever I think about heat or cold, I remember the huge, ancient key being passed around the class. The key was heavy and cold, and the teacher asked us what we thought was happening as we held it. We all thought the cold was spreading from the key, into our hands. Of course the opposite is true—the heat from our hands was spreading into the key—ergo heat always flows towards cold. Useful knowledge in later life—deciding where to place radiators for example.

My best friend was David Barlow and although he

lived on the same council-house estate as me, his family were financially better off—his father had a *'proper'* job. This led his parents to look down on me . . . and my family. I suppose, there may have been other reasons too—my ability to swear for one? Anyway, they (mainly the mother) made it clear I wasn't good enough for their son—it didn't seem to bother James.

We used to play cricket in the street and, inevitably, his mother would have passed by at some time or other and heard me vocalising. I suspect this because David (who I think was always slightly in awe of me), said to his mother once, in my presence,

"Stewart is really good at batting."

To which his mother replied,

"Really . . . ? He's good at swearing as well."

One sunny afternoon at teatime, in the back garden of his house, we were having slices of bread, butter and jam—*Butter and Jam.*

Rationing still existed and she watched me like a hawk, giving me the evil eye as I clearly spread too much of both, on my slice of bread. On the unfortunate death of his father, they moved to a different council house (semi-detached, not in a block like ours), on another council house estate, but still within walking distance for me. David always had expensive toys, but (whenever we were together), was happy to share them with me.

Visiting him at the new house, I found he had now

acquired a Hornby Dublo, electric train set—among other irresistible toys. I think this was a form of compensation for the death of his father. It was permanently laid out on the dining area floor, and of course, I would immediately gravitate towards it. She expressed her disapproval thus:

"That train set's far too convenient there."

"Especially for low-lifes, like you"—she did not say. Surely, she didn't expect him to pack it away every time he had finished playing with it—not even to deprive me of any access to it. Many years later when visiting my parents from London, I was at the local bus stop, waiting for the 'Samuel Ledgard's bus into Bradford, and found myself stood next to David.

We, of course, fell into conversation, and he wanted to know about my life in London. His job was operating a printing press in a Bradford print shop—lots of black ink under the fingernails. I gave him as many glamorous facts about my life in London as I could—some true—some false, in the time available to us. I would love to have been a fly on the wall when he related all this to his mum.

June 1953, the Coronation and Sir Edmund Hilary with Sherpa Tenzing Norgay, conquered Mount Everest—a present for the Queen, and the Commonwealth. The whole school got the afternoon off, and we walked in procession two-by-two, hand-in-hand, me holding

Pudsey

Dianna's (my childhood sweetheart) hand—to the local Pudsey cinema. There to see the film of the conquest. Then there was the day of the Coronation itself. My sister May had bought the first TV to be owned by the Burnett family—it was an HMV in a huge polished wood cabinet, complete with doors—but the screen was not so huge.

I remember one Saturday when, on hearing it had been delivered, I ran the whole way to her house and burst into the living room, to see on the screen—the *Oxford and Cambridge boat race.*

Years later, on the first Saturday of my new life in London, wearing the suit mother had bought me from C&A in Bradford, I stood (along with friends) on Putney bridge. It was a beautiful spring day, and we were watching—the *Oxford and Cambridge boat race.*

On the day of the coronation, all the immediate family, close and distant relatives, and anyone else who could wangle their way in, were sat in May's living room (in three tiers), youngsters on the floor, women on the various chairs—some people brought their own—and the men standing, or sitting on tables, sideboards, at the back. It went on all day.

Even better than the Coronation—as far as we children were concerned—in 1953, the rationing of sweets ended—*What heaven.*

My friends and I ran up to the local sweet shop, and spent every penny we had, on sweets. This became a weekly routine—as soon as the week's pocket money was received, off we ran.

No TV at our house. There was just a large wood-veneered, valve radio, with a huge illuminated station dial and Bakelite nobs. There were many memorable programs the family enjoyed together—'Billy Cotton Band Show', 'Music While You Work', 'Workers Playtime', 'Educating Archie', 'Life With The Lyon's' and of course 'The Goon Show'. One particular favourite that the family enjoyed together, was 'Two Way Family Favourites'—a successor to 'Forces Favourites' that was broadcast during the war. Every Sunday at noon, we would all sit comfortably and listen to the opening theme tune—'With a Song in my heart'. Looking back, it's hard to believe how little decent music was broadcast in those early days of radio, immediately after the war. Consequently, programmes like this were shared, family events.

Friday nights, when mum and dad sometimes went to the pub for a drink, I would be left alone for the evening, with our dog Trixie. I would listen to 'Dick Barton-Special Agent' and then later, perhaps a scary play. This would scare me to death and I would hug Trixie close. It's strange how I would listen to plays, knowing they were probably going to give me nightmares. I suppose like most kids, I did have nightmares. They could quite scary and repetitive—for a while I was afraid of going to bed, knowing the same night-mare would occur.

The radio was also a great source of components for my models and games—valves of various shapes and sizes. They made great 'Flash Gordon' rockets—I used to watch Flash Gordon movies at the Saturday matinee at the Pudsey 'New'n'—for years I thought this was another name like; 'Odeon', until I was told it was—the 'New One', meaning it had been built since the original picture house that still existed, further down the hill in Pudsey town.

The Sunday papers—News of the World, Sunday Express, were a source of titillation for me, with all the semi-naked models. Of course, I could never be seen looking at them. I don't know what possessed me but, on one occasion, thinking that week's papers had been read and cast aside—using a biro, I drew stockings and suspenders on some of the models. Unfortunately, May's Des happened to visit and picked them up to read. I was in deep trouble. Dad gave me a real telling off,

"You dirty little bugger!"

Des thought it was a great laugh. One of our neigh-bours was an agent for the various catalogue compa-nies—Grattan, Kays, Littlewoods. The lingerie sections of these catalogues were an even greater source of sex-ual stimulation for me, but I was never foolish enough to draw in them. They continued as a source of interest, into later life. Even now, I find they still hold some strange appeal to me—whereas, I am completely disinterested in pornography.

When Trixie had a litter of puppies, I was horrified to discover my parents, intended to drown them all. I kicked up a terrible fuss, but they prevented me from entering the bathroom where they were doing the deed. Though I only caught a glimpse, I saw they had a bucket, filled to the brim with water—the puppies were all put in and then a lid was placed on top of the bucket, leaving them no room to breathe. I suppose these days, they would have been taken to the nearest animal shelter—I don't think such niceties existed then. There was no way we could have a house full of dogs, let alone, afford to feed them, but at the time, I was distraught—I could not believe my parents could be so cruel.

May was also the first to buy a radiogram—again this was an HMV, with a cabinet even more massive than the TV. When a Bing Crosby 78-rpm record was played, every ornament and knick-knack in the house, rattled. I had great fun with old or damaged 78s. If you heated them by the fire, you could bend them into all kinds of shapes.

In contrast to all the luxury items, the house was very old, with solid stone walls, gas wall lights and a coal fireplace. Even worse—the toilet was down at the bottom of a long garden, with no lighting and torn news-print hanging on a nail in the wall—no velvet-soft toi-let paper, to wipe your behind on. Freezing cold and dark in winter. An advantage of the gas supply—our house was all electric—was that lighting the coal fire on a cold winter's morning, was a doddle—you just stuck the gas-poker into the coal and away it went. Lighting the fire at our house in the depths of winter—could be a real challenge.

To me, the arrival of TV into our family, while opening a whole new, wonderful world, also had a big downside. Prior to TV (like most children) I found Christmas to be a special, magical occasion when all the family gathered to have a good time—and of course, there were the presents.

There was always keen competition within the family over who hosted which of the days, over the Christmas period. Our house had an upright piano and my sister Sylvia could play, so there would be singing, with eve-ryone gathered around the piano. There were endless party games, and lots of food and drink.

Sometimes there was a little too much drink, and I became aware of alcohol-fuelled disagreements—on one occasion, the men of the family all disappeared up the back garden. I don't know what happened—some kind of face-off I assume, but no one seemed worse for wear.

One time, mum had drunk a couple too many of her

gin and tonics (mother's ruin), and asked May's Des to give her a kiss under the mistletoe,

"Ere Des love, give us one a' them French kisses." Des was understandably horrified, to say the least. I didn't know what a French kiss was.

The next day, I was shocked and distressed to discover mum in the kitchen, dressed only in her underwear and vomiting violently into the kitchen sink. I tried to comfort her as best I could, but it was very upsetting for me. The kitchen sink was the only sink in the house—the bathroom contained only a bath, the toilet was outside and likewise without a sink.

Auntie Elsie and Eva were always the life and soul of Christmas parties. They had an endless list of party games—some quite near the knuckle. One involved an individual being brought into the living room one at a time, blindfolded. They would then kiss the crease of someone's folded arm. On taking off the blindfold, someone would be pretending to be doing up his or her trousers. Another game featured a bowl of warm lemonade and a peeled banana . . . ?

Elsie was my Dad's sister and she looked exactly like him, but Eva was her friend—for many years, I thought Eva was also my Aunty. Eva had close-cropped hair, which was unusual in those days. They always lived together, until their deaths and it seems clear to me now, that they must have been gay. If they were gay, did the family know? Were they even aware of such 'issues'? I certainly wasn't back then.

It was sometime later, that we acquired a TV in our house. A much smaller model than May's, it sat on a small table in the corner, next to the fireplace. It was only Black & White of course. Watching TV with my parents could sometimes be somewhat embarrassing. Programmes were not then pre-recorded before being broadcast.

This meant for instance, that watching drama programmes, it was quite possible for there to be a serious costume malfunction—a woman's breasts might suddenly become completely exposed, especially if there was a bedroom scene involved. Nothing would be said . . . just an awkward silence.

Then there were the various technical glitches that would occur, like microphone booms suddenly appearing in the scene, or a person with a clipboard, appearing on the side of the screen. The news presenters didn't have earpieces—there was a huge Bakelite telephone on the desk, and they would occasionally have to excuse themselves and answer it. Last, but not least, there were the frequent technical intermissions—I wonder how many hours I spent, watching the sea crashing onto a rocky shoreline. Likewise the BBC 'Test card'. Broadcasting hours were limited and the rest of the time, the test card would be showing, for the benefit of installation engineers. Of course, you could turn the TV off, but it had some kind of hypnotic effect, and I spent much time staring at it, wondering when an actual programme might start.

The screens were always quite small and various tricks were utilised to make them seem larger. One was placing a huge (oil-filled) rectangular, magnifying glass over the screen. The screen itself was curved enough, but this contraption made everything so distorted—it was like watching through a goldfish bowl. Another device was a tinted screen that tried to create a coloured image effect. It kind of worked on certain programmes—like 'The Lone Ranger' for example. It made the sky seem blue and the ground earth-coloured.

Then, just as I was getting older and looking forward to being able to join in more of the Christmas games played by the adults—TV changed everything. Now, the family spent the whole Christmas watching *'The Stars Enjoy their Christmas'*—celebrities enacting Christmas celebrations, so you yourself did not have to bother. I was very disappointed. At least initially, they were actually performing live—at Christmas time. Later, with the advent of pre-recording, the stars would be away, sunbathing on some tropical beach, while you were (supposedly) sharing your Christmas with them.

In these immediate, post-war-years, it was only at certain times, such as Birthdays and Christmas, that tasty treats made an appearance. I adored fruitcake, malt loaf, trifle, custard tarts, mince tarts, Battenburg cake, dates and many other delights. The men of the family would all have cigars, that came in aluminium screw-top tubes—these I would use for my model making.

After a brief flirtation with the 'Boy Scouts' at the local church hall, I joined the 'Boys Brigade.' It was more militaristic, with uniforms and lots of marching about. I played Bugle in the band. Although we practised every week, they would never let us play in public. This was a great disappointment to all the band members, as we loved being on the big public parades, with various bands playing. The 'St Johns Ambulance Brigade' was my favourite. They had a particular sound and rhythm, which you could recognise as they approached from afar.

May's Des (who used to play in a dance band when courting my sister), loaned me his trumpet and I would practice in my bedroom. The only tune I knew how to play was the National Anthem. One of the Boy's Brigade 'Officers' lived just up the road from me, directly across from bedroom window. At one of the meetings, he complained to me that, when he was working on his motorbike in the street, he had to keep standing to attention—could I possibly try to learn another tune? Every week, we would parade for inspection. My belt buckle was always the shiniest, and the officers would accuse me of using a buffing machine on it. Why they thought my father needed, or could even afford a buffing machine, I do not know. I kept telling them,

"I use duraglit and elbow grease."

Like many young boys, after school each day I delivered newspapers for the local newsagent. The trouble was, by the time I got halfway through my round, I would always find myself in desperate need of the toilet—every day it was the same. Nowadays, I find I seldom pass up on the opportunity to use a convenient toilet facility. As the Comedian (Billy Connelly) said during one of his routines,

> "Let me tell you about being over sixty. Never
> trust a fart, never pass by a toilet, and, if you get
> an erection, use it, even if you are on your own."

Although as a family, we were not regular churchgoers, sometimes I would read the bible at night. I found some of the stories fascinating and adventurous. Then, I don't know how, I discovered that the Bible was not actually written by God at all, but by several different blokes, hundreds of years after the death of Christ—that was the end of the bible for me. It's like all history—it's written by the victors or those who happen to be in power. They all write their version of reality.

The school system had not finished humiliating me yet. The next came at Eleven-plus time. My older sister Sylvia—the nearest to me in age—had passed

Pudsey

her 11plus, and was already attending Pudsey Grammar School—the first in our family to do so. I of course, assumed I would follow in her footsteps—in what seemed to me, would be a natural evolutionary process—but it was not to be so.

I did not achieve the necessary marks, and the class teacher, determined—it seemed—to inflict maximum pain, embarrassment and humiliation, announced to the class at large, who would, and who would not, be going to Grammar School. I was not alone in being unable to hold back the tears.

So it was not to be the Grammar school, but Primrose Hill Secondary Modern. It had a terrible reputation— it was known among us kids as 'Pudsey shirt rive-rs' (shirt rippers'), and I was filled with dread. In fact it turned out to be an amazing school, so well organised and disciplined. Although I only spent a year there before being offered an examination to enter Art College—it was a thoroughly enjoyable time.

I was one of the founder members of the chess club that was started by the science teacher. In the beginning, we were sharing a single chess set, but by the end of the year, the club was about 60 strong, and all with our own set. Immediately after lunch in the main hall, there would be a stampede for the science classroom, in the corner of the hall.

On a less intellectual slant, I remember the walks home after the day's classes—a long line of boys with the one

in the centre of the line, reading aloud from some 'Bod-
ice Ripping' novel, obtained from I know not where. It
was somewhere around this time I made a shocking
discovery. Out one evening with the local estate gang,
during which there had been some furtive groping
with one of the girls—she just stood there, leaning
against a shed, carrying on a normal conversation as if
nothing untoward was happening, while various boys
groped around under her dress. Later, one of the older
boys explained to me how babies came about . . .

"No!" I exclaimed . . .

"that can't be right, the Queen and the Duke of
Edinburgh don't do that. No, that's dirty."

In those days, sexual education did not exist at all in
schools. Like many young boys, I thought the whole
business was something to be ashamed of and not to
be talked about openly. As I now know, the Queen and
the Duke did do that stuff and . . .

and on more than one occasion.

By this time, I had been introduced—by the same older
boys—to the art of masturbation. It was not easy, to
begin with, but, eventually, I managed to get the hang
of it.

One instructional occasion was in a hollow, in a local
countryside field—a group of older and young boys
like myself—reclining in a circle, like a bicycle wheel
spokes, feet pointing to the centre, attempting to do the
deed. I—among others—was a total failure, but the

older ringleader produced an awe-inspiring torrent. Later, when I had acquired the necessary skill, it became quite difficult to conceal the results of my labours. One day, my mother was washing clothes in the kitchen sink. She said,

"I don't know what's on your vests, but no amount of scrubbing will get it."

I said nothing and slinked silently away. She knew of course, and I knew she knew, and she knew I knew she knew.

Along with friends, I enjoyed going for long bicycle rides to picturesque locations, such as Bolton Abbey some twenty miles away. That was always a good day out, and on the way back, we would stop at Harry Ramsden's fish & chip shop—this was the original and only one at the time. It was located opposite the 'Menston Mental Hospital'—the 'Loony bin' as we would call it. It always seemed slightly spooky and scary to us kids, looking menacingly at us from across the road, as we wolfed down our battered cod and chips. The Name was synonymous with insanity in Yorkshire—if someone said,

"He belongs in Menston".

They were questioning his sanity. We just kept our fingers crossed and hoped that nobody would escape while we were there.

Another memorable bike adventure was to York Bicycle Rally, over thirty miles away, which has been held every year since 1945. The day started badly for me. We were riding at speed down a steep hill, approaching Leeds—the road was, like many, still cobbled, so to avoid discomfort, we were riding between the tramlines, where the cobbles had been tarmacked over—much smoother. Trouble was, I got my front wheel stuck in a tramline and over the handlebars I went—headfirst. Fortunately, it was early morning with not much traffic about. Bystanders picked me up and a kind lady took me indoors and gave me a cup of tea. No bones were broken, and I was soon back on the bike, heading for York.

This was the second time my head made contact with the road while approaching Leeds City. When I was much younger, my mother took me shopping to Leeds and as the bus was approaching our stop, my mother decided—like people often do—to step onto the rear bus platform, ready to make a speedy dismount at the stop. The bus hit a large bump and off I sailed, to bump and roll in the road—the bus continued and disappeared out of sight, round the corner. After what seemed a long time, she came running, screaming around the corner. Then, as on this second occasion, I was completely unhurt.

It was a great day out with lots of things to see and do. On the journey back we were still bursting with the energy of youth, pumping away on the pedals up hills, overtaking Lycra-clad adults—much to their displeasure. We received quite a few curt remarks. Some of these people were riding tricycles . . . ? This struck us as very odd. Surely, tricycles were for children before they eventually graduated onto two wheels. Clearly, older, less able people might prefer tricycles, but this seemed to be a 'style' choice.

Then there was the infamous school sports day at Pudsey swimming baths. One of the girls competing in the 'back-crawl' had a costume malfunction. She was well endowed for her age, and being completely unaware of the situation, swam two whole lengths of the pool. The screams from the girls and cheers from the boys in the audience, were completely deafening. So much so, tutors by the side of the pool were unable to draw her attention to the situation—she must have thought the audience's deafening enthusiasm, was for the display of competitive swimming. I was fortunate to have a grandstand view of all this, as I was competing in the diving event and standing close to the edge of the pool.

Those of us competing arrived back at school later than the others did. I entered the class and slipped into my desk seat, next to the lovely Patricia Craven—she looked at me smiling, as she leaned close, and whispered,

"I didn't know you were such a good diver."

Past Tense

I would have been in seventh heaven, were it not for the fact that (as the audience was rising to leave), two of the older boys had climbed onto the highest diving board, and then onto the back railing—to gain even more height—before doing a synchronised dive, raising a huge scream. I was impressed, but cross—having myself only dived from one of the lower boards.

We had one half-afternoon art lesson a week—barely time to sharpen your coloured pencils, or sort out the tubes of paint. Though limited in time, I was in my element and loved these lessons. On one occasion, I took one of Marie's watercolour paintings along to show the teacher. She was very impressed and said,

"I see where you get it from now"

It was a view of a lighthouse on the Isle of Man, with the sea crashing on the waves. As a child, I used to think it was a brilliant painting, but when I look at it now (having been given it on Marie's death), I see that it's not really brilliant, but still pretty good—certainly better than the oil paintings she did in later life.

Fortune smiled on me then, and I was selected to sit an entrance exam for The Regional College of Arts & Crafts Bradford. The exam was held in Bradford—the Big City. It was spread over two whole days and I had to take the bus alone from Pudsey—what an adventure.

Along with the two girls, I shared a desk with in the art classes—Patricia Craven and Ruth Nelson, I passed. They were both gorgeous, but I never got any-where with either of them. Some people I know will not believe this, but I was too shy and innocent then—I am still a bit shy, but certainly not innocent.

Unfortunately, I am also no longer young.

Past Tense

Bradford

The Junior Department of the Regional College of Arts & Crafts Bradford, at twelve years of age. The curriculum was 50% academic and 50% art based subjects, covering the whole spectrum. Sad to say, they did not expose us to naked life models at this time. Artistically, this was a great education, but it did mean I never got near the finer points of academic subjects, and never anywhere near taking languages, and certainly not A Levels or even O levels. I have sometimes regretted this in later life—my year in France for example—I never really got grips with the language.

I met the late Rodney Turner here. Because of a medical issue as a child, he had lost most of his legs and now used artificial limbs. Despite this, he was still determined to live as normal a life as possible, and he would play football and cricket with us during break time. As I discovered later when we went to the senior college, he was also an ace table-tennis player.

Around this time, I acquired the nickname 'Bunny.'

Billy Kelly, the boy I sat next to throughout the College entrance exam, had pronounced buckteeth. I suppose—as a diversionary tactic—he one day said to me,

> "You've got buckteeth, so I'm going to call you Bunny."

Despite my protestations, the name stuck. At first, I didn't like this at all, and was well pissed with him. But as time passed, I became happy with the name, which stayed with me into adult life. There are people I have known whom, if I met them again tomorrow, would say,

> "Hi Bunny."

I often found, when meeting new people, they would say,

> "Oh, so you're Bunny."

Much more memorable than Fred, or Dick.

Here I was to suffer my final humiliation at the hands of the education system. Having excelled in all creative related—but certainly not maths—subjects, I was made a Prefect for 'Gainsborough House.' This was fine for a while until some no-goods accused me of terrorising some of my fellow pupils. This was not true— I was never in a fight in my life and I was certainly not a bully—more of a coward really.

However, the headmaster chose to believe the stories and I was stripped of my Prefect's badge—in front of the whole college—during morning assembly. Even more irksome, it was awarded to my best friend at the time, Brian. I was terribly upset by the injustice of it all—I just couldn't understand how it had come about. When I told my parents, my father was very supportive and said,

"Don't worry about it; you're better off out of it.

These people will only ever do you down."

I think his working-class resentment of the 'bosses' and other people of authority, was showing. In those days, professionals—doctors, teachers, were still seen as figures of authority and viewed with respect. I was glad and relieved that he was not angry or disappointed with me.

One teacher I liked would introduce the class to George, his stuffed Duck-billed-Platypus—it resided on his desk at all times. He taught the art of calligraphy, featuring 'Chancery Script', and using a broad-nib pen with Indian ink. I enjoyed this, as it complimented my love of lettering and typefaces. One day, he related the story of how—on the death of King George VI, Bradford Council commissioned him to write a letter of condolence, to the new Queen to be—Elizabeth II. The Letter was written on parchment using Purple, Indian ink. Carrying the finished article to college one rainy day—he dropped it into a puddle. To the class' relief, he explained that, as both parchment and Indian ink were water resistant; he was able to wash it clean—

thus avoiding countless hours rewriting it.

Learning to write using Chancery Script, influenced my handwriting style for the rest of my life, and I would take pride in my written letters to friends—especially girls. Then, much later, word processors arrived. Now, I struggle to write at all, and then can barely read what I've written. He also taught English, and I remember clearly a punctuation test he set us one day, writing on the blackboard—*'Time flies you can't they fly too quickly'*—I could not think of the correct punctuation—it just didn't make any sense at all to me. I was a bit stupid. Probably why I didn't get into Grammar School.

Arriving home one day from college, I was mortified to discover Trixie was nowhere to be found. My mother had given her to my sister Marie—she was now living in an old dark and dingy house in Stanningley Bottom and the surroundings were a bit dark and spooky at night. Trixie was to provide company and a form of security.

I didn't really mind, especially as I could visit her as often as I liked. What I did mind was not being consulted at all. It seemed insensitive. I suppose I always thought of her as my dog, but she belonged to the whole family. In those days, parents took whatever decisions they thought were necessary and the offspring had to accept them. Nowadays everything is discussed with the children, the facts of the matter explained and, their opinions sought and (collective), decisions are taken—yawn.

The college organised a holiday to Butlins, Filey, my old stamping ground. This was the first time I experienced the joys of a holiday, free from parental supervision.

Much fun was had by all . . . The escorting teachers generally, left us alone. As much as I would have wished, there was no hanky-panky with the girls, but we boys had a thoroughly good time just being boys. A favourite pastime was playing on the penny Arcade Strike slot machines—this was how we obtained individual, illegal cigarettes.

Going home from college, at the end of each day, I would catch the Samuel Ledgards bus from Chester Street bus station. Bus rides—indeed any kind of transportation, involving movement and vibration—were a source of potential embarrassment to me.

Despite how I tried, it was just impossible, not to get an erection. Then, the moment of dread as my stop hove into view—how to get up and off the bus, without all the fellow passengers, realising my predicament?

This situation became even more awkward when, all too often, a gaggle of Bradford Grammar School girls got on the same bus as me. I would have to endure giggling and half-whispered comments, clearly aimed in my direction. Getting off the bus was now even more of an ordeal. They would be staring and waving from the windows, as the bus pulled away, me hoping there were no visible signs of my erection while trying to appear oblivious to them.

Eventually, one of the girls—who lived not too far away—took a fancy to me. Getting off the bus, I was given a love letter by one of her friends. It contained dolly mixtures and love-heart sweets.

I can't recall her name now, but we dated a couple of times. I recollect these dates consisted of standing in the local telephone box, at the end of our road, on a freezing night—kissing. Years later, when visiting from London, I was in Pudsey town centre with Marie's Des, when I saw her pushing a pram. I don't think she saw me, and I certainly didn't approach her. Des commented that,

"She looked a bit of alright."

I remember the great smog of 1952. For two or three days, the smog was so dense—you could barely see where you were going. It was estimated that twelve thousand people died directly due to the smog—a little more than a third of the number that died during the Blitz - and many more probably died early due to the four days of poison gas that they had to live through. In response to this severe smog, the Clean Air Act was introduced in 1956.

Two years later, the smog was bad again. Travelling home from college on the bus one evening, the conductor was walking in front of the bus with a torch, guiding the driver the way for the last mile, before my home. I don't know what happened to the bus after I got off in Pudsey—its final destination was Leeds. Leeds recorded the highest ever level of sulphur dioxide in the air and pneumonia cases in Glasgow trebled.

Marie and Des had now moved from the house in Stanningley Bottom to a nice, new, council house, in Acres Hall Crescent. Marie bought a radiogram, but this was a 'modern' 50's design, mounted on long, tapered legs. She introduced me to classical music and (to this day), one piece always reminds me of her—Rimsky-Korsakov's Scheherazade. I cannot hear it, without thinking of her.

Celia Cornforth was a tall, slim girl, with blonde, frizzy hair. She wasn't in the same league as Patricia Craven (hey hum) but was good at kissing. We spent every break-time behind some shed, or around some corner, kissing passionately. I learnt a lot about kissing from her. Sad to say, Celia did not happen until after the Butlins trip. However, the next year, the school announced there would be a return visit to Butlins. I was devastated when my parents were unwilling, or unable to provide the money to pay for the trip.

It was probably a good thing as I could quite well have got into trouble with that Celia—as I was now into the potentially dangerous age of puberty, perhaps my parents had it figured as the wise course to take.

Bradford

I did get to go to the Blackpool illuminations with the school and Celia . . . Lots of heavy petting on the coach journey, but nothing too untoward. When we arrived in Blackpool and everyone was getting off the coach, she drew me to the rear, full-width seat of the coach and said

> "Lie down with me; it doesn't matter if your prick goes near my crack!"

I was slightly taken aback, but complied with her instructions.

When at the normal school leaving-age of fifteen, I was offered a place at the senior Art College, a certain amount of 'discussion' took place, within my family. *Why should I not leave college, get a job and contribute to the family, as my elder siblings had all done . . . ?*

> "We all had to do that." was heard.

I can't remember which one of my siblings said that, so I give them all the benefit of the doubt.

In our neighbourhood, this was the normal course of events for children, at this point in their life—they left school, got a job and continued living at home—contributing money for board and keep, until the day they married and (if lucky) then moved into their own home. Dianna was still living in the next block to us, and she was recommended to go on to further education. Apparently, her mother said,

> "I've kept 'err long enuff. It's 'err turn to keep me now."

Past Tense

She ended up as a Pudsey supermarket checkout girl. Years later, I was surprised to learn she was married to a distant relative of mine, so was now *Mrs Burnett*. Some years later, I met them both at my mother's funeral.

Fortunately, the body of opinion fell in my favour, and it was agreed I should continue my 'Artistic' education, and so I progressed into the Senior Art College—naked life models—yeah!

I lost contact with all my local friends when I started at Senior Art College. They, not having had the same moment of good fortune as myself, were now working in relatively mundane jobs—building sites, checkout counters and—print shops.

I don't remember how it came about but, around this time, the local food and sweet shop on the Waterloo estate asked me to do their shop sign. I thought this was a great test of my graphics skills, and a chance to earn some money. Unfortunately, about halfway through the job, I dropped my precious, adjustable set square from the top of the ladder, and it broke into pieces—it cost more than I received for the job.

My first encounter with Len was during enrolment day at the Art College. We were all in a large room, and one by one, our names were called out and we had to walk up to the front and sign the Register. The Yorkshire cricketer (and Pudsey dweller), Sir Leonard Hutton was still a household name at this time, and inevitably, Len's full name was Leonard Hutton—he walked to the front to the accompaniment of a chorus of giggles. Poor Len. How cruel of his parents to choose that Christian name. Len always seemed very self-conscious and walked with a kind of sideways slant, as if to see what was going on behind him. He would also walk close to walls with the same kind of defensive posture. It did not help his confidence that he also suffered from bad eczema. None the less, he was a nice guy, and we got on just fine. He would later become a 'Clan' member in London.

The first year was 'Basic Design'—this was a forerunner of what would eventually become University PreDip and Foundation courses. Art subjects were not then, degree courses. During that first year, we studied every art and design related subject—photography, fine art, sculpture, all forms of printing, colour theory, graphic design, metalwork etc. The plan was that, at the end of the year, you chose your preferred subject to focus on for the last three years, up to graduation.

I still wanted to become a graphic designer, or 'Commercial Artist', as they were then called, but the tutors felt I had an aptitude for 3-Dimensional work, and suggested I should take up Industrial Design. I was attracted to machinery and would spend hours in the college library, looking at magazines showing JCBs, large cranes, earth movers and anything that was good-design, and functional.

Past Tense

This was not an available subject at Bradford, so I was steered towards Exhibitions & Display—a stopgap until I could go on to study Product Design at the Royal College of Art, in London. The second year was dull and depressing—Window Display—the world of coloured felt and the staple gun, with (upon graduation), the joys of window dressing at Brown & Muffs, Bradford—ugh.

Brian Stewart was my best friend at the junior department, and continued to be so in the senior college and eventually, in London as a 'Clan' member. We met Dot during this time, and she and Brian quickly became an item. He would relate his sexual experiences with her—I was still very much a virgin.

With hindsight, at the age of fifteen, we were a bit too young to be undertaking an art education curriculum, (which would eventually become a University degree course). There was a lot of time wasting, fooling around and flirting with the girls when the tutors were not around.

The Life Drawing classes could be particularly distracting for us boys—especially if the model happened to be both female, *and* attractive. There often seemed to be a plague of weak bladders, requiring frequent visits to the toilets.

Being in the senior college meant that (for the first time), we had the freedom of self-determination, to come and go as we pleased—to assume responsibility for succeeding or failing at our chosen subjects. It took a while for us to realise this. As one of the tutors said,

"You lot have still got Junioritis!"

Things became more serious after the first year. Then, the arrival of a new tutor Myer Lacombe, direct from the real world of design in London. He made exhibition design much more exciting and introduced interior design as an unofficial subject—for those of us who were interested.

There was a backyard in the college, where the Pottery and Sculpture departments were located. It had direct access from Morley Street. One day, we were amazed to see a brand new Austin Mini parked there, sparkling like a jewel against the backdrop of black, soot stained paving and building stonework— the vast majority of Bradford was soot black. To us, it was as if something from the future was plonked there. None of us had ever seen one before—it was possibly the first one in Bradford. Such a design icon and still going strong today.

The 'Liberal Studies' lesson, was both fascinating and scary for me. Fascinating, because I was introduced to music I had never heard before—'Music Concrete', 'Live Songs from the Chain Gang' for example, as well as a wide range of classical music. Scary, because I was a working-class vocational student and this lesson mixed us with the middle class, diploma students. These students lived in semi-detached—or even detached houses—not council blocks. The kind of houses I would feel intimidated by when delivering papers in my younger days.

From time to time, we would be called upon to stand up and give an opinion on one subject or another. One such subject was military conscription, and I had to say my piece.

I was one of the lucky ones—a year older, and I would have had to do two years of military service. Two of my fellow students were not quite so lucky. Liberal Studies were the domain of Madam Andrews—a large, imposing woman, who would sweep around wearing a black cloak and hat. She was fond of declaring,

"I am not Miss Andrews and I am not Mrs Andrews, I am Madam Andrews!"

David Hockney was a couple of years ahead of my friends and me, but we became acquainted when drinking in the local pubs after college. Him being a conscientious objector, when he graduated, he had to do two years (in lieu of National Service), scrubbing bodies in St Luke's hospital. Sometimes in the evening, we would be drinking in the Queens hotel just down from the college, and David would turn up with a test tube containing pure alcohol. He would pour drops into each of our pints of Tetley's bitter.

I can tell you, this was a very effective mix.

College 'Rag days' were great fun, especially the Rag

Ball, at the 'Queens Dance Hall'. One year, we devised a particularly childish prank—although it seemed a great idea at the time.

We invented a sect named 'The Dodos' and we posted silk-screened posters all over Bradford, stating—"The Dodos Are Coming." The highlight of this farce was a plan to string a banner between the Odeon cinema tower and the Alhambra Theatre dome—across Great Horton Road. On the Friday night, before the Saturday procession, and under cover of darkness, two of us climbed onto the building roof, dressed in our cloaks and dodo masks.

After about twenty minutes, the police apprehended us. It was humorous to them and extremely embarrassing to us, as they sent us on our way. What plonkers we were.

The Rag Day charity procession was always fun and then there was the Ball in the evening. One year, Peter and I, paired up at the ball. We had by now discovered smoking—thinking it glamorous. Peter would say as we entered the bar,

"Okay, take a long drag and then blow it out
slowly, just as we enter."

Peter turned out to be a questionable friend—the kind it might be said of, "with friends like that, you don't need enemies." We hadn't met up until the second year of college when he transferred from textiles to our department. His father had abandoned him, his sister and mother. I think this had created personality issues in him. He always had to be top dog, in any situation and was happy enough if that was the case. If not, he could behave unkindly. Over time in later years, I certainly had the occasional run-in with him, about women usually. He invariably seemed to have the best job, more money and the nicest clothes, than the rest of us. He was certainly a talented designer—but flawed. I often felt in later years, that he was reworking other people's ideas.

At college, we all used to roll our own cigarettes, sometimes adding filters. We also experimented with making Menthol cigarettes. We would go to this amazing shop—Rimmingtons pharmacy in Bridge Street in Bradford centre. We could buy menthol crystals there and add them to our roll-ups. Very cool—but probably not so healthy.

The bar was busy and it took ages to get a drink, so we hit on the idea of not buying just one drink, but four at a time—we would then lodge them in our various jacket pockets—this was not a good idea. By the end of the evening, I was soaked in whisky—my preferred drink, at the time.

The Student Union would organise a late night bus, for the end of the ball. What an ordeal that was. It was as if the bus travelled around the whole of West Yorkshire, before finally dropping me off—and even then, I would have to walk a mile home. I was always drunk, trying hard not to vomit. To this day, the smell of whisky makes me experience a wave of nausea.

My first venture into archery was with Peter. We went down to 'Brown & Muff's in Bradford, and each bought a wooden longbow and arrows. This was new to me, but Peter had done it before, at a club, so he provided instructions. We would go up on Baildon Moors and have a fine old time, shooting at anything and everything. To simulate live game, we would release balloons, to blow across a valley, while we frantically released arrows at them.

I remember Brian and I once spent a night at Rodney's home. We spent the whole night awake, listening to Frank Sinatra's 'In the Wee Small Hours' LP. His vocal timing is just incredible. It was amazing to see how Rodney moved around at home—he would take off the limbs and scamper (at speed), around the house, up and down stairs, just on his hands. Consequently, he had great upper body strength.

He expressed an interest to come camping with Brian, Dot and me—we had a favourite spot on the Moors, outside Skipton. It was a little-wooded valley, enclosed by a rocky escarpment, with a stream coming down, off the moors. An idyllic spot we visited from time to time. We were dropped off by local bus, some distance from our destination and we started hiking through the fields and woods. It was a miserable, rainy day and at times, we were slogging through chest-high

Heather. Consequently, we were all soaked through to the skin.

At lunchtime, we stopped for shelter in a ruined barn—just a few beams to shelter under. Baked beans were soon bubbling on the primus. Rodney, sitting there said,

"So this is camping? Bloody Hell!"

Off we set again, and towards the end of the day, we reached our usual campsite. I just don't know how Rodney did it—I was completely exhausted. Brian and I went ahead and got the tent pitched in a temporary location, ready for the others. We then all piled in and promptly, fell asleep. The next day was gloriously sunny. We moved the tent to our usual spot by the stream and started drying all our clothing. During the day, Rodney was sitting on the top of a dry stone wall, sketching. His limbs, complete with trousers and shoes, were leaning against the wall to dry, directly under him, but with a significant gap. It was amusing to see the expressions on the faces of the few hikers, who happened to pass by.

He clearly enjoyed this rain-soaked introduction to camping, because he joined us again, but this time, we left the road at a much more convenient location. I certainly would not have wanted to do that hike again. Graham and I were both in Exhibition & Display at college. There were woodwork-evening classes for adult City & Guilds students, and on the occasions we stayed working late we would sometimes chat with them. One of them had made this beautiful classical guitar, and Graham and I were inspired to do the same. We spent ages making a mould to form the curved sides of the guitar body, and after buying the various veneers, we met up in his mother's kitchen. Using a kettle of boiling water, we attempted to steam bend the veneer around the mould — it did not work and the veneer splintered. It was a hopelessly naive endeavour.

Robert was a fellow junior Art School lad. He was quite short in stature and not happy with the rough and tumble of the other lads. I have a memory of him in the locker room, timidly undressing for P.E. and visibly shaking with anxiety and apprehension. It seemed odd that while we all spoke with Yorkshire accents, Robert, spoke like a proper toff.

It was even odder when years later, on one of our trips up north to visit family, a group of us went to pick him up from his home and met his family. He had several brothers and they were all typical Yorkshire lads, and along with his parents, all had very broad Yorkshire accents. How Robert had developed such a gentrified accent at twelve years of age, was a complete mystery to me. I guess that's one reason why I never felt as close to Robert, as I did with the other 'Clan' members.

While at college, I worked weekends and holidays at a local bakery — 'Jesse Stevens Gold Medal Sunshine Bread.' My job was van boy, so I got to ride all over

Past Tense

West Yorkshire. Not an unpleasant job, but tiring, with long hours. I had to get up at five o'clock in the morning and walk over a mile through fields to the bakery. It was usually cold, dark and wet. Also, the fields contained a great many cows that I had to pick my way through, trying to avoid the steaming cowpats—I was not always successful. The cows always seemed interested in me—perhaps they thought I was the farmer arriving to feed them. One of the perks of the job was that—at the end of the day—I got to pilfer treats, such as custard tarts, Eccles cakes, mince pies and doughnuts etc. This was sometimes with the van driver's permission, but sometimes without.

When I became seventeen, I could no longer work on the vans, as they took most of the little wage I earned, in tax. So Brian and I then started work in the actual bakery—during the summer holiday, doing night shifts.. Working on the ovens was hell—the heat was almost unbearable. Though we were naked under our white boiler suits, after a while, we would be standing in a large puddle of sweat. You could not stop—you had to keep up with the tempo of the oven. Brian left, but I carried on a while longer, until I could stand it no more. It wasn't just the horror of the job bothering me, I was also feeling lovesick for a certain Andrea Robinson—a fellow art student. We spent lunchtimes together, in the student's common room. She was blonde with startling blue eyes. I found it wonderfully erogenous to stroke the back of her knees and she didn't seem to mind. Then, she had given me the heave-ho and I was not feeling happy about it.

One day I just bailed out and went to the locker room to change back into my street clothes. The supervisor accosted me there and began berating me for letting my fellow workers down—I think he meant himself, as he would have to fill in for me. He said,

"We fought the war for people like you and this is the gratitude we get."

I did not care—I was out of there for good. I went straight to Andrea's house and rang the doorbell. Her father answered and said she wasn't there. Maybe she wasn't. In any case, he invited me in and took me into the garden, to show me his greenhouse. He was kind to me and showed me his plants. One I remember would react to your touch—it would shrink away from you. I was impressed. I learned she was adopted then. I wonder if she was hiding in the house while I was there. I never did get back with her and later I was well put out to see her at one of the college dances, with some other bloke—it was fancy dress and she looked amazing in black tights, with no skirt.

One Saturday evening, a group of us ended up at a party. It was quite lively and we knew a few people there. After a couple of drinks, a female I knew came up to me, with this other girl in tow—Judith Unwin was her name.

Past Tense

"Hi Stewart, this is my friend Judith."

"Oh hi." I said, and then drifted off, to another part of the room. Shortly after, the same duo returned.

"Hi Stewart, this is my friend Judith."

"Oh hi again." I said, and then I suppose I got the message . . .

Before much more time had elapsed, I found myself in an armchair, with Judith on my knee, necking passionately. We stayed there for the rest of the evening until I had to catch the last bus home. Subsequent dates consisted of meeting at the 'Alassio' coffee bar and then we would end up on a bench between the Queen Victoria Memorial, and the WW1 memorial. We would sit there snogging in the dark, trying to keep warm, until I had to get my last bus home from Chester street bus station.

This was the beginning of a relationship which brought limited physical pleasure and a good deal of emotional distress. She was an ex Bradford Grammar School girl, with a good home background—her parents lived in a large detached house—so was intelligent and well spoken. She was not slim but well endowed. It lasted for a year or so, with lots of heavy petting, but no actual intercourse. She started University up in Durham and I would sometimes go to visit her for the day—getting the early morning coach from Leeds and returning on the last one at night. Apart from the occasional spot of sightseeing, the day was mainly spent in her room. Again, with lots of heavy petting.

One weekend, Peter and I hitch-hiked up to Durham together—I don't really know why Peter came. We arrived late at night and got talking with a gang of students. We thought, being all students together, they would offer us some form of accommodation, but no such luck. It was too late to visit Judith, as she was living in Halls of Residence. We ended up sleeping in workers' building-site hut. We were able to brew some tea but had to sleep on the floor. Next day, we visited Judith—much to her surprise. The next night we had to sleep in one of the unfinished buildings, on the University grounds. To keep warm we wrapped ourselves in some insulation material that worked fine, but Waking next day we discover that it was fibreglass—and very, very itchy.

On our following 'Rag' day, we decided to get revenge for the Durham Student's inhospitality. Five of us drove up in Graham's Dad's car—he was away at the time. We had prepared all manner of insulting posters—very juvenile, but worse, we took lengths of timber and non-reversible screws. With these, we sealed the University doors, with everyone inside. Ridiculous behaviour for which we should have been punished. It created quite a stink—they knew it was Bradford people, but could not prove who, so the fuss passed.

Past Tense

Occasionally, during holidays, Judith visited my home and stayed the night. She was to sleep in my bedroom, while I slept on the living room sofa. Of course, once my parents had gone up to bed, the frolicking would begin and go on all night. She would go upstairs just in time before my mother came downstairs in the morning.

On her last visit, straddling me on the sofa, she eventually managed to lose her virginity. But that was it—as soon as the deed was done, she stopped the proceedings—just as I was beginning to enjoy it. I've often wondered if my parents knew what was going on downstairs. She then went to Paris for a few days—something to do with her college French course. She was picked up by some gigolo and had lots of sex. I suppose it's quite possible that she picked him up.
To be told this when she returned was incredibly upsetting. She had given me a hard time all along, so this seemed like the last straw.

However, I don't know how, but one evening we found ourselves at the flat owned by Dot's Dad. We were in bed together, naked and after some kissing, she performed fellatio—apparently, the gigolo taught her this trick—and then she straddled me. Being so inexperienced I didn't stand a chance and had to immediately withdraw and climax. To say she was angry is an understatement.
Later, sitting at the kitchen table, with Dot and Brian,

she leaned close and whispered to me,

"You're not a man, you're a shirt button."

That really, finally, without any doubt—was that. She was now the experienced women and me, the pathetic virgin. That night, to avoid me, she was sleeping in the same room as Brian and Dot. I went in and suggested she leave them in peace, to do whatever they desired. She agreed and we ended up (platonically), sharing a bed in the other room. In the middle of the night, Brian was shaking me awake—Dot's Dad had arrived back unexpectedly. Judith ran to get in bed with Dot, and Brian jumped into bed with me. The next morning there was the big inquisition. Brian and I were very nervous, as her Dad was a bit scary. But in the end, all was well.

As it happens, I did see Judith again. She came to visit me in London one weekend, and on one of my visits up north, I ran into her (by accident) at a party. To say the least, neither of these occasions were enjoyable.

Graduation time came in 1960 after four years—seven years total, including the juniors—and I was nineteen years old. It was time to join the real world. Our friends and fellow students, Doug, Len, Pete, David and Robert, all promptly departed for London—the centre of the design world—but my friend Brian and I, unbelievably decided we were going to travel around the world. We got a job for three months on a Bradford construction site, helping to build a 'British Homes' store in the city centre. The Council were ripping the heart out of Bradford, destroying all the old cobbled streets and demolishing the lovely old Victorian, soot-Black buildings—remnants of the woollen industry which had previously, made Bradford so prosperous.

As labourers, the work was exhausting, consisting of every dirty heavy job going. Huge articulated lorries would arrive loaded with thousands of building-bricks. Nowadays, these are unloaded by the pallet, using the lorries own hydraulic lifting arm. Then, they all had to be unloaded by hand. You split into pairs—one of you on the lorry and the other one on the ground. The bricks were thrown at you, three at a time, and you had to catch them with your bare hands. The concrete was delivered in cwt bags (112 lbs), twice the permitted maximum weight of bags today. You had to pick these up off the floor, up onto your shoulder, in one swift action—or drop it again! No such thing as 'Health & Safety' then.

The easiest job I had was drilling holes in the concrete slab ceiling to take A/C ducting support bolts. The compressed air drill blew a steady stream of concrete dust into my face and the only protection I had was a handkerchief tied around my face, and of course my flat cap. No face-mask, no hard-hat, no high-res' safety-vest. One of the bricklayers was a brute and the foreman was even worse. He had a piggy nose and bad teeth. Another of the bricklayers was a nice little man and he befriended a bricklayer who was black. This was quite unusual in Bradford then, and he was subjected to racist abuse. One day, there was an altercation and the little chap threw off his flat cap, and picking up his brickies hammer (with sharp spike), challenged the brute to a fight. It was scary for a while but fortunately, no blows were exchanged. The company boss then located the little man and his black colleague to work in a different part of the building site. I can't recollect any other Black Africans in Bradford at this time, but there were many Pakistanis. I believe that today, they form over 20% of the population. They were brought into the country to work in the wool industry, which created great wealth for Bradford.

It seemed to me that working on a building site consisted mainly of moving materials from one location to another, only to have to move it again, to a different location. Eventually, we quit the job and off we set with our rucksacks, hitching down to London— Dot's father dropped us off at the A1 London Road. He wished us luck and said,

"If you get invited to dance with any rich, old la dies, don't hesitate."

We spent a few days in London, with the clan, and then off we set hitching our way to France. We made it as far as Paris—our naivety was amazing. In my rucksack, I even had an aluminium collapsible, hunting bow and lethal looking arrows—where we imagine we'd be hunting our food, is beyond me. We surely would have starved to death.

When the reality of our childish endeavour set in, Brian and I had a terrible argument—he wanted to return to his girlfriend Dot, but I wanted to continue—but I was also feeling very apprehensive about the whole stupid idea. We were sharing a hotel room together, but other than that, we ignored each other. I realised, I also wanted to quit, but I was glad he made the decision for us—allowing me to retain the moral high ground.

London I

So, it was home to Bradford—tails between our legs. After a short while, we hitched down to London again, to join our friends—the 'Clan'. Our final lift on the journey—a large van with a very uncomfortable bench seat—dropped us off on Fulham Broadway. It had been a long tiring journey down and we were very hungry. Into the nearest fish shop we went, and ordered,

"Fish 'n chips please."

The woman behind the counter rattled off a list of names that meant absolutely nothing to us.

"Fish 'n chips please," I said again.

Once more the unintelligible list of names. Finally, we realised she was listing the names of all the available fish—cod, plaice, haddock, rock and so on. In the north, we just ordered fish 'n chips. Fortunately, 'cod' rang a bell—so cod and chips it was. Ah, the first of many mysteries in the big city.

We stayed with our fellow Bradford boys for a few days, before we found our own bedsit in Parsons Green. We were only there for a week or two, before a room became available in the Onslow Gardens house, with the rest of the Bradford crowd—all seven of us together now—the 'Clan'.

There was so much work around—I got six job offers within a week.

The job I took was with an exhibition contractor in the back streets of Hammersmith, behind the Olympia Exhibition Halls. They also had a side-line in chauffeur-driven limousines and the design office was above the garage. The summer was hot, the garage smelly, the job terrible, the boss horrible—a real barrow boy, who smoked huge cigars and shouted,

"Oi, you!" whenever you tried to sneak past his office.

The chief designer was a nice bloke—he was a friend of Myer Lacombe, which is why I took the job. Unfortunately, the job was not such a good one. I was paid ten pounds a week, from which I had to pay three and a half guineas a week rent, for the bedsit I was sharing with Brian. One evening visit to the pub and jam sandwiches for lunch all week. There was a box on the studio wall full of brown envelopes, each containing a design brief. Most of these were speculative and if the design proposal was successful, the fees were included in the construction costs. You went to the box, opened the envelope, read the brief, designed the scheme, put it back in the finished box. This involved producing an 'artist's impression', along with a simple plan. This was the last you ever saw of the project. I never saw anything being built or visited a construction site. After seven months, I had learnt everything I possibly could about producing perspective, artist's impressions, and quickly found another job. They offered me more money to stay—but no way. The new job was with Rapier Design—an exhibition design group within the Roles & Parker advertising agency.

This was better. I got to produce construction drawings and specifications, and better still, to visit the contractor's workshops, to monitor construction. I was also able to supervise site installation at the different exhibition halls. I worked for various major clients such as Plessey and Smiths Electrical Instruments and had some exciting and interesting times.

Their products ranged from electronic components, so small (you had to display them under a magnifying glass), to large hydraulic controls, such as the ones used to control the swivelling jet nozzles on the Harrier Jump jet. I saw the first public flight at the Farnborough Air Show. One takes this sort of thing for granted now, but then it was a weird thing to see. I also saw the maiden public flight of the Vickers VC10—a beautiful aircraft, so huge at the time, it seemed to block out the sky. Ultimately, it lost out to the (not so beautiful), Boeing 707.

My boss, the clients and me, went for lunch in a marque—there were white linen tablecloths, expensive looking cutlery, and flowers on the table. This was a completely new and nerve-racking experience for me. Which of all the pieces of cutlery was I supposed to use first? it was only later that learned the 'work in from the outside' rule. Just choosing what to eat was a challenge. I went for the fish—Northern lad, fish 'n chips—except the fish had *no batter and came complete with bones and head*. I watched what my betters did and muddled through, somehow.

The seven of us lads from Bradford Art College—Doug, Len, Robert, Peter, Brian, David and Me—were known among new London friends, as the 'Clan.' We were all broke but had some great times. We were living in bedsits in a large house in Onslow Gardens, South Kensington, just across the road from the 'Anglesea Arms' pub. This was our local for a long time, even after we had moved to Earls Court. These early years were great fun, and we had a terrific time on little means.

The caretaker was not very nice, but the landlady was Dora Bryan, famous for her roles in the 'Cary On' films. A good Northern lass.

We certainly couldn't afford fancy holidays, but some of us used to going camping during summer weekends and holidays. We had a favourite spot on the beach at Newhaven, where we would pitch our tents under the cliffs on some solid ground above the shingle beach. We had a lot of fun there. I once spent a blazing hot weekend alone there—with my new 'Voigtlander' 35mm camera, that I wanted to try out. One holiday, we camped there for a while and then we set off hiking along the coast—past Seaford and Cuckmere Haven, then up and over the Seven Sisters. A breath-taking stretch of coastline and quite a hike. Early evening, we finally arrived in Birling Gap, one of the few places you can get down to the beach. Into the pub, we stumbled, and ordered,

"Five pints and five Cornish pasties, please."
That was the first round, and five more pints and pasties later, we were feeling full of the joys of life. This was late season and as we were the only visitors, the locals took kindly to us. They invited us to play 'bar skittles' with them and that was great fun.

When last orders were called, this beautiful woman stood up and sang 'Bali Hai' from the movie 'South Pacific'. Corny I know, but we were transfixed. She was Adele Leigh, a familiar face on TV. Down onto the beach, we staggered and spent some time dicing with death, among the large waves crashing on the beach. We slept on the beach in our sleeping bags that night. Waking up Sunday morning to a beautiful day we found ourselves surrounded by sunbathers. We joined them for most of the day, before catching a local bus to Eastbourne, and then a train back to London—work the next day.

October 1962 and the Cuban missile crisis. Doug, Len, Pete, Brian, Dave, Robert and me, all recent arrivals in London and eager to continue our exciting new lives, were sat around the table, in one of the Onslow Gardens bedsits. We were all listening to a transistor radio (no TV for us in those days), wondering if it was all going to end before we got started. This was a genuinely scary period in our lives and there was such relief when it ended. We all thought Kennedy was fantastic. Barely a year later we are once again, sitting in horror, around the same table, having learned of President Kennedy's assassination. I was thinking—why do the good people get assassinated, not the George Wallaces, the de Klerks and the Bothas, of the world?

Jean Mallinson was a friend of Judith and part of the Bradford circle. Same background as Judith and quite sexy. A fellow student at Bradford college, Geoffrey Gee, was quite small in stature, but good looking and (like many small men), assertive by nature. He was successful with girls and certainly, not a virgin. At times, it seemed to me I was the only virgin in my year, if not the whole of Bradford, if not the world . . .

He recounted to me that; Jean Mallinson was what is referred to, as a 'prick teaser.' Even so, on one of my

London I

return visits to visit family, Jean and I became an item. A long-distance relationship, with many passionate letters passing back and forth—no sex. Then, a week-end London visit was arranged . . . full of excitement and anticipation—I bought a new shirt, with starched cuffs, cuff links and detachable collar.

Meeting her at the head of the Kings Cross tube station escalator, I was disappointed to see she had come with my Brian's girlfriend—Dot.

So, this was no longer my special weekend, with Brian (hopefully), making himself scarce, as much as possible.

We slept together in my single bed, for two nights—during which, she requested that I kiss every inch of her *naked body*. When on the second night feeling—un-surprisingly—aroused, I attempted to move towards intercourse. She was horrified and angry and said we were finished—our relationship was over.

I was shattered and Geoffrey Gee's words came to mind. This second, failed relationship left me feeling emotionally scarred, and nervous of women.

Then, a new girl called Caroline arrived in the house. She was studying ballet at the Rambert Company. She was a Goldie Horn look-alike and sexy. One evening after we had all been drinking in the Anglesey Arms, I retired to my bed. She was trying to get into bed with me, but I was resisting. Eventually, I said,

Past Tense

"You can get in with me but, I'm not going to have sex with you."

Well, she did get in with me and we did have sex. All my anxiety about women and sex seemed to then, well . . . disappear, never to return.

To this day, I do not know what possessed me, but one evening I took her for a meal at Bertorelli's by South Kensington tube station. After food and wine, I ended up asking her to marry me. We had only known each other for five minutes, but she accepted. Announcements to all the 'Clan' and then celebratory drinks in the Queens Elm.

Of course, this was sheer idiocy, and a few days later in a state of inebriation I told her, and everyone present, I could not go through with it. She didn't seem terribly upset. She was probably relieved. All part of a game, I think.

It turned out she was—to say the least—a bit flighty, and managed to have sex with just about all the 'Clan.' Then, one day she announced she was pregnant and the question was who is the father? Ever the sharp one—Peter immediately asked her when her period was due, and after a quick calculation, eliminated himself from the equation. The rest of us dummies looked at each other, not knowing what to say or do.

She certainly had put herself about. It was all a silly game on her part. She was not pregnant and eventually—to our relief—she disappeared from our circle.

London I

But, bless her . . . she got my relationship with women, back on the rails—from the viewpoint of sex, anyway.

While not a fellow art student, Rosie had been part of our Bradford social scene. She was beautiful and elegant, and on one of my Northern visits, I took her to the cinema on a (sort of) date. Visiting her parents' house one time, I was amazed when she took me into the study—books everywhere. The walls were lined with books. With the exception of the 'Children's Encyclopaedia' and 'Sporting Handicap', there were no books in my parents' house. In those days, there were lots of 'travelling salesmen' knocking on doors, trying to sell complete sets of 'Encyclopaedia Britannica' and they could be very aggressive. They were out of luck at our house. No way could my parents afford that, even with the weekly doorstep collection of a few shillings.

We did exchange letters for a while, but nothing came of it. Sometime later, she visited London and spent the night sleeping on the floor of the bedsit I was sharing with David. Preparing for bed, she was kneeling on the floor by the fireplace, brushing her waist-length hair. I was laying in my bed watching, catching glimpses of her naked breasts, through her hair . . . I was afraid to make a move—months later, she told me she was just waiting for me, to reach out a hand . . . Years later, our paths would cross again.

Again, in 1962, I was to experience another 'Smog'

event. It lasted three or four days, but not quite as bad as 1952, but bad enough. It was bitterly cold and walking up Earls Court road in the mornings, it felt like my ears were being bitten. You could feel the pollution in the air as you breathed. A scarf wrapped around your face was the only protection. Life in bed-sitter land was spent huddled around a gas fire, periodically inserting coins into the gas meter.

It was at Rapier I first met Kerry Hallam, a graduate of Central School of Art. I don't know how he became an exhibition designer, but it's what he was hired as. He was five years older than I and much worldlier, but we became friends. We then acquired a new Chief Designer—the late Jim Downer—and he took us both under his wing. He was such a dynamic individual and a keen sailor. Kerry and I were frequent visitors to his home and we sometimes helped with the DIY jobs he couldn't manage himself, him having the use of only one arm—the result of Polio as a child. We would go sailing with Jim and his wife Wendy, whenever they chartered a yacht for holidays.

Kerry was a bit of a rogue, particularly with regard to women. Later, I was fortunate to enjoy the 'crumbs' from his table on a couple of occasions. At Rapier, I had my first encounter with Champagne and Caviar. A reception was organised for all the companies' clients. Our office was on the top floor, so I was delegated to meet guests in the ground floor lobby and escort them up in the lift. On one particular lift load, I made a complete arsehole of myself by saying,

"Looking forward to the champagne and Caviar?" This to people who regularly attended such events. I felt very silly the moment the words left my 'northern hick' mouth.

Anyway, after all the guest had been duly escorted up to our floor, I got to sample the Champagne and Caviar. Very nice, although I don't think at the time, I knew what Caviar was—if I had—I might not have been tempted. After a time, I became a dab hand at champagne receptions—discovering the delights of Champagne and 'Buck's fizz'. That 'Buck's fizz' can certainly sneak up on you, when you ain't looking.

Around this time, I was experiencing periods of anxiety. It was distressing and I didn't know what to do about it until I read 'The Conquest of Happiness' by Bertrand Russell. I learnt the process of analysing my daily life to see what, if anything was troubling me—usually I would realise that there was actually nothing to worry or be anxious about, at all. If there was something (work related say), there was no point in worrying about it until the next day, when you could address the situation.

While sharing a double bedsit with David, in Earls Court, he invited me to go to the cinema with him—he had bought tickets to see 'West Side Story', hoping to take a particular woman he liked. Unfortunately, she declined his invitation. He was a nice person and I was sad for him. I remember queueing outside the cinema, in Leicester Square. That was always fun—the endless procession of buskers, the bags of roasted, hot chestnuts and (on this occasion) it was snowing, creating a lovely pre-Christmas atmosphere. No one queues outside cinemas any more, which I suppose is convenient, but not necessarily good. I still love roasted, hot chestnuts, especially at Christmas and especially when mixed with Brussel sprouts.

One Friday evening, having left work with two weeks holiday pay, I was in a snooker hall with the clan, prior to us all going on to a party, when I discovered my wallet had been stolen—three weeks wages were gone. My friends went on to the party, while I returned downhearted, to my Earls Court bedsit.

Every cloud has a silver lining—on returning, I found three house residents, sitting in the communal kitchen. One was a rather attractive lady—Alison, whom I had not encountered before. We talked for hours, before retiring to her single bedsit and having a mind-blowing, sexual experience.

This Silver lining turned out to be somewhat tarnished. Visiting the office urinals, some days later with a work colleague, I remarked I was in some discomfort passing water and had a discharge.

"Oh", he said, "It sounds like VD to me."

I was mortified and took myself off to the Clinic at

London I

Hammersmith Hospital

Sure enough, it was Gonorrhoea. I was given a quick injection in the behind and told I'd *"be ok in a few days"*. In my naivety, I felt as if I had the plague—afraid I would infect my roommate, my work colleagues, the world. In my anxiety, I told Mr Court the studio manager whom I hated, as he was never nice to me and had absolutely no idea of design. He was sympathetic,

"Oh, I saw lots of this in the army, during the war. No need to worry, we men know how to deal with this sort of thing."

When I told Alison, she was horrified and apologetic, saying,

"I wondered why I had a discharge. I think I got it off the ski instructor I slept with on my holiday."

Duh!

I was surprised when the studio secretary confided to me later, that she too had just caught Gonorrhoea from a ski instructor on her recent holiday—I do not think it was the same instructor . . . I think they are probably all as bad as each other.

Alison and I continued our relationship for a few months, until she immigrated, to Australia. This was convenient for me, as I decided the relationship didn't have much future.

Jim Downer and Kerry had both, previously moved on to other pastures, leaving just me and another guy—Ian who had diagnosed my VD in the studio toilets. I had a good eighteen months in this job before they had the audacity to fire me. I had been working 24/7 on the Plessey head office showroom and my normal routine had got a little shot. I came in a little late one morning, missing a meeting with the design director and a client—so he fired me.

On my own initiative, I had just designed the stand for the most important Plessey exhibition of the year and only the account executive had seen it. He loved it. I took the design with me when I left the building . . . .
Poor Ian was tasked with trying to remember what the design looked like.

I then decided I would take time out, brush up my portfolio and try for the Royal College of Art. It seemed like a great idea, as I was spending a lot of time socialising there anyway—one of the clan, Doug Binder from Bradford, had gone there to do fine art, hopefully, to follow in David Hockney's footsteps. Through Doug, we socialised more with Hockney and had some great, cheap (and sometimes free) times at the Royal Art College parties and the Film Club. A couple of films I recall—'Wages of Fear' and 'The Seven Samurai.' Also the Luis Bunuel/Salvador Dali film 'Un Chien Andalou.' Hockney said to me one evening,

"I'm having a party at my place on Friday. Come
and bring your friend."

The friend in question was Peter—a pretty boy, but not gay.

London I

One Saturday morning, Peter and I went down King's Road—along with Carnaby Street, this was the epicentre of the sixties, trendy new clothes scene. We each bought a jacket and trousers from 'His Clothes'.

This was my first visit to this completely new and exciting world. The trousers were flared of course, while fitting tightly at the hips and thighs. My jacket was Mustard corduroy. The shop measured your inside leg, and while you went off for a beer, they altered them. After the drab clothes I'd worn until then, I felt terrific wearing this ensemble—terrific and sexy.

After spending several months on the Dole generally messing about, playing Five-card brag with friends until the early hours of the morning, I decided I didn't really want to go back to college after all. I was weary of the frugal living—a diet of boiled cabbage and potatoes, among other delicacies. I just wanted to get on with work and life. I managed to pick up a few freelance projects and eventually got a job with architects Leslie Gooday & Associates. The original intention was for me to work on designing the Interiors of a large, new hotel on the South Bank, a project they had won via a design competition. As it was never built, I ended up doing yet more exhibition design.

Never the less, it was interesting stuff, for clients such as UKAEA, British Iron & Steel, Rank/Bush/ Murphy, Irish Tourist Board etc. Their office was at the top of Sloane Street in Knightsbridge, which was great. I could visit art galleries and Harrods at lunchtime and sometimes, on summer evenings I would stroll across into Hyde Park and play Crown Green bowls with friends.

On other evenings, I might walk down Sloane Street to Victoria and play snooker with Rodney, who had now joined us in London. Over the years, he and I played a lot of snooker together. I think we must have played in almost, every snooker hall in London.

Rodney had a dreadful 'Tippen Delta' three-wheeled invalid car, but he drove around London as if it were a formula 1 car. There was really only room for him, but by lying under the bonnet, head to the front, next to his feet, I could travel with him. Hairy—you were lying in darkness, just a few inches from the road. Still, it meant we could go places together and it sometimes, provided a much-appreciated lift home, after a late night party.

The story goes, these Tippen death traps, were actually more expensive than a Mini to manufacture, but the government wouldn't provide adapted Minis, because then everybody would want one. They were dreadful and condemned invalids to a solitary existence—when they were travelling anyway.

Sadly, the company moved the office to Putney. Not much fun at all and the transport links were terrible. Graham (who had now joined us in London) Peter, Len, Robert and I were living in West Hampstead, in a

London I

large flat, on the top floor of a mansion block. This was the start of a great 'party season.' Rosie was now attending a Dance and Movement College in Weybridge and she would come up to London at weekends, with some of her fellow female student friends. Graham had a large Telefunken, reel-to-reel tape recorder, on which were just about all the top pop bands of the time—all the Beatles tracks, Searchers, 'Love potion No.9' and 'Needles and Pins', spring to mind, among many, many others.

I had never been able to dance in the traditional sense. When at the Art College balls, I was always one of the blokes standing around the edge of the dance floor wishing I had the courage (and the skill), to invite one of the girls dancing around their handbags, to dance with me.

With the arrival of the 'Twist', it was a new world—everybody could do the twist. Of course, the twist was a bit limited in movement, but it opened the door to a kind of free-form improvisation it seemed I was good at, especially when I had a few drinks under my belt. Chrissie was one of the Weybridge girls I became particularly fond of. However, I never managed to have full intercourse with her, during this time. Our paths would cross again later.

Friday nights were always drinking night and we would all meet straight from work, in one of our favoured pubs. Everyone had to buy a round of drinks, so we could consume a significant number of pints before 'Last Orders' were called.

Then back to the 'Everest, 'our favourite Indian restaurant in West End Lane. One evening, they played a trick on me—being a naive northerner, I thought that Bombay duck sounded like an interesting meal and would be a welcome change from my usual Mutton Vindaloo. With great ceremony, they served me with this revolting little piece of dried fish.

The kitchen staff were all looking through the kitchen door window, having a great laugh. Fortunately, they had also prepared my usual Vindaloo.

Some nights, there would be some unruly types eating there. Their trick was to start an argument and then rice would be thrown around—you had to be ready to duck. In the general chaos, people would run out of the restaurant without paying for their food. Lowlife scum, displaying their lack of respect.

We became friendly with the staff there, especially the owner's son. On his birthday, he invited us to an Indian restaurant in Leicester Square. The food was fantastic and free.

One of the guests was another Everest regular—a woman whose name I can no longer recall. She came back to our flat and I ended up sleeping with her. I regretted this the next day. Suffice it to say, she was not my type at all—but needs must.

Having been on the dole part of this time, I had

London I

signed on to do GPO Christmas post, along with hundreds of students and other 'down-on-their-lucks', like me. It just so happened I ended up with a couple of empty mail-sacks, which I just stuffed into the bottom of a cupboard in the kitchen. The landlord, who clearly gained access to the flat from time-to-time when we were all out, saw the mailbags and called the police. This was shortly after the 'Great Train Robbery', and next, we knew, there was a gang of detectives and police officers banging on the door. After some explanation, they all departed, looking slightly disappointed. It was also at this time that we were burgled, twice, and my camera was stolen — the only thing I had of any real value.

Not having had sex for some considerable time, I was feeling desperately horny. One evening, I was in the flat on my own when Odette turned up on the doorstep. She was sort of on the periphery of our group and much older than we were. We had originally encountered her and another woman, back when I was living in Earls Court, with David. They turned up at our bedsit with one of the clan, after pub closing time. At one point she was sat next to me on a bed when she said,

"I won't cook you an amazing breakfast, but I'll
make passionate love to you all night!"

I was somewhat taken aback by this, and the fact that she was a good bit older than me. Consequently, I did not accept her kind invitation—I then heard her repeating the same pitch with Peter—and he did.

I guess they were what's known as 'cougars' these days. I think she was feeling horny too, because before long she persuaded me to take a taxi ride with her, back to her place. She was all over me in the back of the taxi and I was feeling embarrassed, thinking the driver would see something untoward. Next morning, I left her place for work, regretting the night before and feeling, somewhat tarnished.

Peter, Graham and Len, now decided they were going to immigrate to Canada. This meant, those of us remaining, had to find somewhere else to live. I ended up down in Seagrove Road, Earls Court, staying temporarily with Helen, my new girlfriend.

The friendship with Kerry, Jim and Wendy continued, and on one of our sailing holidays, we crossed the English Channel in a little, four berth 'Crusader' class, yacht—doing the 'Cherbourg Run', as it was known in yachting circles. Cherbourg was where the 'Queen Elizabeth' liner stopped for passengers and 'Duty-Free', before proceeding to New York. The Cherbourg run for English yachts was about obtaining cheap booze and perfume. We set sail in the afternoon, from Gosport.

There was little wind and the engine was running the whole way. I was sitting on the main boom, holding the mainsail out, to try to catch what little wind there was. Twenty hours later, coming into Cherbourg outer harbour at dawn, we lost a boat hook overboard, and while trying to retrieve it, we (inadvertently), jibed — the result being one of my thumbnails was partially ripped off by the boom, as I tried to protect my head.

Eventually, after twenty hours of night-time sailing, I found myself in a queue at the local hospital. Standing there, I was swaying from side to side. 'The sailor's Gait' — my body thought I was still on the boat. A band-age and a Tetanus jab and I was done. From calm to blowing a gale — we were holed up in Cherbourg for three days until we had no choice but leave — Our yacht charter was due to finish the next day.

At the crack of dawn, with storm jib and mainsail well reefed, we set sail. We had all been taking 'Kwells' sea sickness tablets, which were effective but they had now run out, and we had to use the French 'Drama-mine' tablets. These had strong side-effects and turned us into drowsy zombies.

The wind dropped slightly, so we decided to change the storm jib — OMG. The bow was rising and falling about twelve feet. Then, of course, the wind got up again . . . . We arrived outside Cowes, Isle of Wight, nineteen hours later, in the middle of the night and we all collapsed, exhausted into our bunks.

Two hours later, the Customs launch pulled alongside and dragged us all — bleary-eyed — out of our bunks. They thought we might be smugglers, coming in under cover of darkness. We had anchored outside Cowes, as the harbour was full and difficult to navigate in the dark. When we tried to raise anchor and relocate the boat to its berth inside, the anchor just would not budge. It was fastened solid.

Jim went ashore and phoned the owner and he came by to help—but no luck. We attached a marker buoy to the anchor chain and cut free. Back in London, we heard from the owner—a heavy floating barge crane had raised the anchor to find it was attached to a huge WWI naval warship anchor. He also related a dramatic and moving story—he had chartered the sister Crusader yacht, to a vicar and his family. They had undertaken the same journey as us, but slightly later in the day. Subsequently, they had been caught by the storm, that we had just managed to miss.

After hours of trying to enter Cherbourg, against the tide and storm winds, they had all gone below and closed the hatches. There, they prayed as a family—vicar, wife and two children and fell asleep exhausted, leaving themselves to the mercy of . . . whatever?

They awoke the next morning and went on deck, to find they were sailing close off the English coast, and all was relatively calm. The yacht had somehow sailed itself back across the channel—one of the busiest shipping lanes in the world. The owner was euphoric—I think the vicar and his family were quite happy too—

London I

"Praise the Lord."

Sunday morning, the day after returning from this holiday, Kerry turned up on my doorstep—my bedside actually, as Helen and I were still in bed, having spent much time celebrating my safe return. He said he was going to drive down to the south of France to visit a friend, and invited us to join him.

Never one to turn down an exciting or interesting opportunity, Monday morning I phoned Lesley Gooday and told him I wouldn't be returning to work for another week—he was not pleased. The three of us set off for France in Kerry's Mini. On arriving there, I was introduced to Peter Crofton-Sleigh. He was living in the village, renovating houses for English owners. Here, I was also introduced to (a friend of Peter's), Valerie Singleton who (coincidentally) was also visiting.

This was awkward as from the first moment, there was a strong sexual attraction between us. I looked at Valerie, Valerie looked at me and Helen, looking at us both, knew exactly what was happening.

We were all on Pampelonne beach one day when it was suggested we all try water skiing. Valerie was a regular snow skier, so was quite good on the water. The rest of us were hopeless. The instructor told us if we lost balance, to fall forward. Of course, we all fell backwards, and we then realised why it's best not to fall backwards—instant enema. After several failed attempts at skiing, on leaving the water, we all rushed to the toilet.

I'm ashamed to say I parted company with Helen and took up with Valerie. When Kerry and I returned to London, Helen stayed on with Peter. This turned out to be a satisfactory arrangement for them both.

Back in London, I was overwhelmed by a sense of deep dissatisfaction. My life seemed so unfulfilling and dull. After being exposed to this other world of Ramatuelle, St Tropez, sunshine and beaches, London bedsitter-land just did not cut it anymore. I thrashed around, trying to think what I could possibly do to change my life for the better, or at least make it more interesting. I considered the merchant navy, but they do not take just anybody, and it seemed I had no skills of interest to the VSO—design is such a useless profession in the real, nitty-gritty World.

It's true that time heals all, and with Valerie Singleton's help, I managed to regain my equilibrium. The relationship with Valerie lasted for a year or so. I was living in a dreadful bedsit in Lillie Road, Earls Court. The communal bath was filled with rubble, I had to wash, and shave, using a basin of water heated in the kettle. The only heating was a paraffin stove, in the middle of the floor. The contrast between this and spending nights, weekends in Valerie's sumptuous, two-floor apartment, featuring polished wood floors and Persian rugs, was to say the least dramatic. She was five years older, so I guess I was her 'Toy-boy.'

London I

The flat had central heating, the beds, duvets, the bathroom a bath — in which we once had sex. She used to read to me in bed — from 'Winnie the Poo' and 'Wind in the Willows'. She had a soothing voice — consequently, a major source of her income was from TV advertisement voice-overs. She was no longer working on 'Blue Peter', but on our first date since France, she invited me along to the BBC studios where she was presenting late test transmissions of colour TV. A few people in London had colour TV sets, and after the evenings normal B&W transmissions had finished, these colour tests would begin. I stood in the control room looking at Valerie through the door, and seeing the same image on the control room monitors. At the time it seemed magical to me — we had sex that night.

I met several of her BBC colleagues, actors and news presenters. At first, I was slightly in awe of them, but I quickly realised that they were all quite ordinary people — in fact, some were really quite boring.
Valerie threw an election night party at her place. It was quite exciting, as it was the year that Harold Wilson and the Labour Party swept into power.

Valerie had this lovely old Morris Minor convertible, which was a joy to ride around in. I can't remember why — I certainly wouldn't have suggested it — but we ended up driving all the way up North, to see my parents in Pudsey. The top was down and Roger Manton rode with us, sitting in the back. Up the A1, we went—it was sunny but windy. Valerie's visit caused a minor stir on the street, and (of course), my parents were very impressed. Inevitably, my Dad pulled his little party trick—any new visitors would be offered a cup of tea, and when they tried to add sugar from the bowl, they would be puzzled to find no sugar was being added—Dad's magic teaspoon had a hole in it. The sugar would escape back into the bowl. Embarrassing. More embarrassing, was Dad asking Valerie,

"E Valerie, what do you think to our lad then?"
I don't recall her reply.
After the year, I decided time was up. We were (of course), poles apart in terms of lifestyle and beliefs. I remember attending a Royal Festival Hall classical concert with her once. There were some minor (nobody), royals in the royal box, so they played the National Anthem—I chose not to stand. However, she, of course, did. We agreed to part ways, amicably.

While I was living in Lillie Road, Rosie came up from her Dance School in Weybridge. We went out for drinks and then back to my room, where we had sex for the first time. She then promptly left to get the last train back to Weybridge. Strangely, a week or so later, Chrissie who was also at the Weybridge School, phoned me at work and said she would like to come up and see me,

"That would be nice", I said. "What about this weekend?"

99

London I

"No, now," she said,

"Tonight."'

"Oh . . . okay, see you later."

She stayed and we spent the night thrashing around in bed, but without actually having full intercourse—I don't know why. She left early next morning, to get back to school.

Alan Hughes became part of our circle and he was great fun, especially when he adopted a heavy Welsh accent. Alan was a successful fashion designer and designed all the clothes for Emma and Steed in the 'Avengers' TV series. On Saturday afternoons (when he eventually arose from his bed), he was known to say,

"I have absolutely nothing to wear tonight."

He would then sit down and make from scratch, a pair of trousers and a shirt. These items of clothing were sufficient for the coming evening's clubbing activities. He could be difficult at times and once I said to him, in frustration,

"Alan, you're such a pain in the arse!"

Him being homosexual and me not realising what I'd said until I'd said it, we both collapsed in hysterics.

When Brian and Dot got married, they asked me to be the photographer. I had just bought a new, Pentax 35mm single lens reflex camera to replace the stolen one, and this would be the first opportunity to use it. Outside the Parsons Green Church, I had all the guests posing individually and in groups. I climbed a tree and took shots looking down on them.

When I had taken over thirty-nine shots—it was a thirty-six exposure film—*I became worried*. On opening the camera, I discovered (to my horror), the film was not engaged in the winding sprocket.

So, after profuse apologies to all and the film re-engaged in the sprocket—and still in the tree—I ran through all the various posed shots again. When I had (again), taken over thirty-nine shots, *I definitely became worried*. On opening the camera, I discovered (to my absolute, absolute horror), the film was not in the winding sprocket.

How embarrassed is it possible to be I wonder, before it becomes total humiliation? Later I discovered the sprocket rotated in the opposite direction than I had assumed. Now my policy is always 'RTBM'—'Read the Bloody Manual.' It was a relief to find some guests had cameras and had taken photos.

Roger Manton (another Bradford boy, who joined us later) and I got a flat together in Streatham. Dreadful transport links, but—being South of the river, cheap. This was such an improvement on the Lillie Road bedsit—for a start, it had a bath. We decorated as best we could but had little money and furniture. We had some good times there and there were the occasional female guests.

I got on well with the Chief Designer at Gooday's, he

London I

was a good designer and together, we worked on some interesting exhibition projects. I learned a lot from him, but it seems the company always lost money on his projects, and so eventually, he was asked to leave.

His replacement and I hated each other, on sight. He was not a good designer at all, and very overbearing. One of us had to go, and of course, it was yours truly.

Ramatuelle, Var, France

Fortune smiled at me for the second time, and within a couple of days, I received a phone call from Kerry. He told me Peter Crofton-Sleigh needed help to renovate a house in Ramatuelle, for an English client.

So, I gave two weeks-notice and was out the door. I was happy to see the boss and the chief designer were—conversely—not happy.

But, it was also a sad time for me as, after the breakup with Valerie, I had met a lovely lady called Patsy Pollock. She had gorgeous green eyes and kissing her made my knees knock—she would get the shakes too. She introduced me to the music of (among others) Bob Dylan and Miles Davis. Certain Dylan tracks always remind me of her.

We had a full relationship, which was great, but I always felt (perhaps) she was a bit out of my league—I think she controlled the relationship. Surprisingly, while I was working my two weeks-notice, Dorothy Evans decided she wanted to bestow her sexual favours on me, which she did twice at the Streatham flat.

However, men must do what men must do . . . so I left. Well I thought I'd left—having bid farewell to all my friends, next day I went to meet Peter at his girlfriend's house in Notting Hill. Arriving there, he said,

"Oh . . . we are not leaving until tomorrow."
What to do? Lacking an invitation to stay with them, I left my rucksack there and wandered, aimlessly off. After all the farewell drinks and speeches, I could not face going back to any of my friends, so it occurred to me, to phone Valerie. I explained my predicament, and although we hadn't seen each other for some time, she invited me to spend the night with her. And very pleasant it was too.

The next day, Peter and I drove off in his WWII, canvas top, Wiley Jeep. Slow but exciting—the autoroutes did not exist then, so it was the old two-way roads, braving the terrifying French drivers. On the way, we stopped off in St Michele just outside Paris for a few days, to do some work on the house of Michel Saint-Denis, the French actor, theatre director, drama theorist and WWII Resistance broadcaster.
While we there Peter said,

"Ok, I'm not going to be doing all the cooking, so Watch closely and I'll teach you some dishes."

Past Tense

I had never done any serious cooking before, so paid close attention and managed to learn some basic dishes—Risotto, Ratatouille, Chicken casserole and Omelettes etc. The idea was to take turns, cooking on alternate days.

We arrived in Ramatuelle a couple of months before Christmas 1965, so while it was still relatively mild during the day—it could get cold at night. The summer season had ended and the tourists had all departed. The village was beautiful and so wonderfully, different from anything this northern 'hick-from-from-the-sticks', had experienced before. I was introduced to John, who was working with Peter at the time. John was living with Margaret, a somewhat senior, but rather attractive woman.

The story goes thus—John had arrived in Ramatuelle with his wife, who had promptly run off with Margaret's son. So . . . John moved in with Margaret. Fair swap?

Once again, I was plunged into the world of physical labour. We were to build an extension to the existing house (a small, one-up, one-down), out into part of the area that used to be the prison cells, located to the rear of the village chateaux. The extension was to add a large living room on the upper floor, with two bedrooms on the lower floor. My first task was to go into the ruined cellar and shovel the tons of rubble—from the collapsed roof and upper floors—out through a small hole in a wall. At the end of the first day, I crawled out of there on hands and knees, declaring,

"I can do no more today."
and collapsed on my bed.
Peter and John looked at each other, but I was past caring. When I first started, the hole was at my feet. By the time I had finished—after several days—the hole was above my head. Then, each shovel full had to be carefully aimed at the hole. If I missed, it would come raining back down on me. This was undertaken with the traditional French shovel—pointed blade and a long broom-type handle. It took some getting used to.

I gradually built up my strength, and (eventually), could put in a full day's shovelling. When I reached the lower level of the old vaults, I was able to crawl through the rubble into the rear of the Main Chateau building. I discovered this huge banquette room, with an enormous table containing all kinds of plates, dishes, cutlery and other objects, all covered in untold years of dust and cobwebs. It was if people had hurriedly left for some reason, never to return. It reminded me of the scene from the 1946 Charles Dickens' film 'Great Expectations'—with the dust and cobweb-covered wedding feast that never happened.

I spent all of Christmas there alone, as Peter and John returned to London, to be with family for Christmas. There was no way I wanted to return to London so soon. I was completely besotted with the village and more than happy to stay. After completing the few tasks Peter had left me, I spent most of my spare time sketching around the village.

On Christmas Day, I rode the old 'Solex' bicycle (Peter had provided for me) down to Pampelonne beach and sun-bathed for hours, among all the deserted beach huts. It was like paradise to me—I could not believe my good fortune.

The house—11, Rue de Centre, was right next to the boulangerie, and I would wake up each morning to the smell of freshly baked bread. A trip down the stairs for croissant and pain au chocolat to be washed down with fresh, strong coffee.

Open log fires in the evening, with sometimes wind and rain beating against the shutters. Blues, classical and folk music on the record player, and of course the free red wine. Never was much achieved in the evenings.

The free wine resulted from Peter and me spending the odd Sunday mornings tending a small vineyard below the village. It was owned by local villagers Marie Claire and her husband. They lived in the house directly across the narrow street from us, so narrow you could almost reach across at first-floor level and pass things to each other. Marie Claire was a loud and buxom woman, with a habit of exposing too much flesh through the window. When in our kitchen, I had to avert my eyes occasionally, because, if she caught your glance, she would greet you loudly, exposing even more flesh.

During the first few months living and working in Ramatuelle, I spent many contented hours sketching the village, from all angles and perspectives. I don't remember now how many I did—the interior walls of the house were covered with them. In the summer months, when friends came to visit, I gave all of them away—visitors always wanted a souvenir of Ramatuelle.

Peter was an eccentric gentleman, and as he declared one evening—during a philosophical discussion,

> "By preference, he was a Jack of all trades, and
> master of none."

This was in response to my stated yearning to be consumed by some creative passion, or occupation. I have since come to believe he was right, I too feel the same way now. Although the 'Snow Patrol' lyrics,

> *"For once I want to be the car crash,*
> *not always just the traffic jam,*
> *hit me hard enough to wake me"* . . .

resonate with me. I would still like to be consumed by something creative, or adventurous.

Peter was a keen Astronomer and had a huge, motorised, eighteen-inch, mirror telescope. It was located down the hill from the village, in the garden of a local French friend and abstract artist, also called Pierre. Being motorised, it could track the movement of the heavens and allow the taking of long-exposure photographs. Development and printing of photographs were done in our tiny bathroom. Pierre spent all summer in the villa, painting furiously. Then, during winter, he loaded up his mobile home and drove around France, selling the paintings.

He had decided he wanted to build a bigger art studio in the garden and Peter agreed to let me help with the foundations. What Peter had not told me, was that Pierre was a nudist. A bit strange, to be digging foundations with someone's bare arse in your face—especially a blokes.

One afternoon, while I was working there, Peter turned up (in an agitated state), with some French people—they were Customs Officials. Some local had ratted on Peter, saying the telescope had been brought into France, without paying the relevant import tax. Peter was upset—he didn't know who had contacted the authorities, or how they knew the situation. The officials inspected the telescope and then they all went back to the village.

When I had finished work for the day, I returned to the village. The customs officials were still there, sitting around the kitchen table, questioning Peter. They weren't unfriendly—just doing their job I guess. They all admired my many sketches, mounted on the walls of the house.

They relieved Peter of almost all the money he had left.

Ramatuelle, Var, France

Things were then tight for a while until we could get another advance from the English owner of the house, we were restoring. Peter arranged for us to have credit at the local village shop, owned by Madame Arnaux—so we could continue to eat. She was a nice lady and as we were now considered part of village life, was happy to help us.

I loved that feeling of being a local—not a tourist, and have always felt that way since—never been one for package holidays.

During my time there, I had a brief (one day) career as a fashion model . . . David Hamilton who (at the time), was the art director for the Paris fashion store 'Printemp' had a house in the village, and would sometimes come down at the weekend. He turned up one Friday with a gaggle of beautiful, young models, for a location shoot. Having finished work for the day, I was sitting at the kitchen table reading, with a glass of wine to hand. David knocked and entered with a beautiful young model, asking for Peter. I told him Peter wasn't there and he started to leave, but, as they were exiting the door, the young model said something to him, causing him to pause and re-enter the kitchen. He asked if I might like to do some modelling for him—I immediately had visions of Pampelonne beach and 'Riva' speedboats, surrounded by gorgeous young girls.

Much to my chagrin, it did not turn out like that.

Past Tense

The day's shooting took place in the streets, around the village, with me wearing various shirts and slacks combinations. The only 'beach scene' consisted of me lying on a pile of builder's sand. The locals (who knew me by now), were leaning out of their windows and having a good old laugh. Still, I got the equivalent of £30 for the day, which was a lot of money to me in those days.

David became a regular visitor to our house, sometimes for meals—although I think my cooking was a bit beyond him. I tended to put everything I could get my hands on, into whatever the dish was.

I was usually in a state of desperation, regarding the various young models he would arrive with. Drinking with him one evening, in the Cafe de l'Ormeau, he said,

"I don't get it on with the girls; I prefer watching
them fooling around, together!"

There were times when I felt lonely—especially on a Friday or Saturday night—thinking of all my friends in London, and wondering what they were doing for the weekend—visits to the pub, or perhaps a party. I would sometimes ride up to the top of the hill above the village and look out over the coastline towards Toulon—feeling isolated and miserable.

However, I always reassured myself I was doing something different, positive and exciting. Something I would have regretted for the rest of my life if I had passed the opportunity by—you always regret things you didn't do, not the things you did.

One afternoon, early in the year, I was relaxing after work at the kitchen table (and yes, with a glass of wine to hand) when in walked Kerry and three girls—direct (by Mini) from London. One of the girls (Ruth) was an American.

She was from a well-known American folk singing family—had a flawless voice, and played guitar well. Kerry also played guitar and had a okay voice. Their plan was to make money, busking around the St Tropez restaurants and bars.

One of the girls took a fancy to me, and I reciprocated—Anita was her name. We hadn't got beyond kissing and cuddling when (to earn some extra money) Peter, John and I returned to London, to work on the interior decoration and restoration of a house Michel Saint-Denis had just bought in Pimlico. Off we set in the jeep, with a trailer behind containing all John's possessions—John was going to work on the house, but he was not going to return with us to France. Peter and John took turns driving and we did the journey nonstop, to save money. I snatched as much sleep as I could, in the back. In London the work on the Pimlico house went well, and I learned a great deal about decorating—skills, which have stood me in good stead, later in life.

I stayed with Brian and Dot in their Finsbury Park flat,

and we had some nice times together. While in London, I used the £30 I had earned modelling, to pay for the fretting and restoration of a banjo, given to me by Rosie. Dot, who was a fashion designer and ace with a sewing machine, made me an amazing, waterproof cover for it. It was a happy period in London, seeing all my friends again. Evenings in favourite pubs and the occasional party.

Peter had changed the Jeep for a second hand canvas-top Land Rover and with two friends of Peter's— the late guitarist and blues singer Davy Graham and his girlfriend—we set off to return to France. Just outside London, near Gravesend, the engine blew up. It was a cracked cylinder head. Fortunately, a friend of Peters lived in Gravesend, and he towed us to his home, offering hospitality to us all.

A new cylinder head was purchased by Peter's girlfriend friend in London, and dispatched to us by train. We spent three days there while we rebuilt the engine, out on the roadside. All the hours spent with Des paid dividends for me here.

Off we set again, with our two passengers. Davy was trying to kick his heroin addiction and I think the trip to France, was part of the therapy.

Peter, Davy and I sat up front on the bench seat, playing guitar and banjo and singing our way down to the South of France. The poor girlfriend spent the whole journey sat in the back, squashed into the tiny space left by the rear tailgate, with only flapping canvas to protect her. To earn a little more money, Peter had agreed to deliver a large engineered-model steam-locomotive for a wealthy Englishman. It was to be dropped off at his apartment in Monaco. We got there in the middle of the night, but the owner wasn't there and we couldn't get access to the apartment, as the chef from the owner's yacht was in there—with a woman. Leaving the engine in the corridor, we were invited (by the steward) to spend the night on the yacht, anchored in the harbour.

Waking the next morning at 5am, I was amazed by the panorama of Monaco, surrounding the harbour. It was just after the F1 Grand Prix, and all the roads were still set up for the race.

Davy Graham said to the steward,

"I'll come back sometime and play for you."

"Oh no," said the steward, "They don't like that sort of thing around here."

We had breakfast ashore in a waterfront café and then drove along the picturesque coast road, back to Ramatuelle.

It was now spring and the weather was beautiful.

As soon as I arrived back in Ramatuelle, Kerry asked me to go for a walk with him. He explained that, while I had been in London, he had fallen in love with Anita. He asked,

"How do you feel about her? Will you be bothered

if I pursue the matter further?"

As I hadn't had much time to get to know her and didn't have any strong feelings at that time, I said,

"No problem."

Of course, when (a couple of days later) she asked me to meet her, I was reminded of how beautiful she was. We went swimming and she was wearing a particularly revealing bikini. A knitted affair, a type I hadn't seen before, and it became ever so slightly transparent, when wet. She explained she had absolutely no feelings for Kerry, other than friendship.

It was me she wanted—so we became an item. Unfortunately, I could not get her to have sex with me—everything else, but not full intercourse. I guess I was grateful for whatever favours she was willing to give.

As a group, we had some lovely times together, driving around in the open top Land Rover. Trips to St Tropez on market days, sitting outside the Café des Arts in the Place des Lices, drinking cold beer and playing chess. Eventually much to my dismay, she disappeared off back to England—for gawd's sake, the months were ticking by and I was not having any sex.

Due to my enthusiasm for sailing, I loved strolling along the harbour, admiring the luxurious yachts anchored there. My favourite bar was the Le Gorille, from where I could admire the boats and watch the world go by. We would sometimes visit St Tropez and catch Kerry and Ruth performing around the restaurants at night. Francoise Sagan, and many others could be seen passing by, on the way to some exclusive club or other. The Spanish Flamenco guitarist Manitas de Plata—relatively unknown then—was also busking around St Tropez. Occasionally, he would come and play for us, as we were friends of Kerry. His guitar playing was out of this world.

Life there was pleasant, despite the (at times), hard physical labour. We had free, live music every evening after dinner. Peter played guitar, cello, tuba, and I was learning to play American style folk banjo. This was 1966—the year England won the World Cup. I wasn't at all interested, as I was suffering from a terrible toothache at the time. The next morning I was in the dentist's chair in St Tropez and he was saying to me,

"Félicitations pour avoir remporté la Coupe du Monde."

Having virtually no French, I couldn't understand him.

"World Cup!"

he finally said—my poor academic education was now biting me on the bum. It would irritate me when friends visited and I said to them,

"Do you speak any French?"

"Oh no", they would reply. A few days later, they would be jabbering away—like a native.

"I thought you said you didn't speak French?"

Past Tense

"Oh well, I did it at school."

Working on the house was a fulfilling experience and I would not have missed it for the world. Ramatuelle is just a few kilometres from St Tropez and overlooks the Gulf of St Tropez and the Pampelonne plain with its beaches. It is (or at least was) unspoilt, compared to say Gassin, which is visible on the hilltop from St Tropez and therefore fell victim to the rich-chic set. This was before the Beaux-Art-Committee started protecting the French heritage.

The house was located right against the central church clock tower, on the back of the original Chateau and was extended into part of what used to be the 'Cell de Garde'. We were consequently in the highest part of the village, and the views from our front patio, were magnificent—almost 360 degrees, from Toulon around over the Gulf of St Tropez, with the snow, covered peaks of the Alps behind, continuing around towards Toulon, until only the peaks of the hills behind the village, obscured the panoramic view. I absolutely loved it there. It was hard physical work, but this was offset by so much beauty, fun and interesting people. I learnt many new practical skills working on the house and these have served me well in the years since.

The village is part of protected French heritage, so all work had to be historically correct. Many of the materials we used were in fact, 15th century, reclaimed from derelict ruins in the surrounding hills—the roof and patio tiles for example. All the external walls tended to be natural stone or rough cement rendered. All internal walls were natural stone or finished with white Plaster-of-Paris, quite different to modern gypsum plasters.

Cutting doorways through three feet thick stone walls was a challenge. I loved building with the local stone. When the money ran low (between client payments), we would have to scavenge for materials. We dug sand from a local, freshwater riverbed—you cannot use the salty stuff from the beach.

We also took on other jobs, such as taking the jeep and trailer up the rough 'Cork' trails into the hills above the village. All the surrounding hills are covered in cork trees, usually harvested by Algerians. The cork being so light, we would come back down the trails, with a load of cork so huge, you couldn't see the trailer under it. We took it through the village square and down to the main road, where it was transferred to large lorries from the cork factory.

Kerry and Ruth were often asked to perform at private parties. They performed at Brigitte Bardot's birthday party among others. On one such occasion in a villa overlooking St Tropez, Peter and I were invited along with them. The villa was being rented by Ricky, a minor American actor based in France. He specialised in gangster-type roles—he looked just like the classic American gangster, which was a bit scary. The party and the villa were terrific, complete with a large swimming pool.

I made the acquaintance of an attractive English girl (Wendy Wilberforce-Smith), a debutante, who was working as an au pair, for some toffs in town. We hit it off and she agreed to come up to the village to see me. This was a bit awkward at the time, as Ricky (the party host), was obviously keen on her too.

We met again and became an item. We had a lovely evening together on Bastille Day. There were music and dancing in the Place des Lices. The big music hit at the time was Frank Sinatra's *'Strangers in the Night'* and everywhere you went throughout St Tropez, you heard it playing. Quite romantic—but I never did get to have sex with her—was I ever going to get my leg over again?

One night I came as close as you can get, but it was not to be. We were in bed together in the house, both naked and she was admiring my manhood when we were interrupted. The problem was, at the time I was sleeping in the alcove off the kitchen-living area, separated only by a curtain—another close encounter, but without success.

Ricky (sort of) became a friend, in that he attached himself to our circle. He enjoyed chess, so we played together, sometimes at his villa, or in the village. He was always enquiring how I was getting on with 'WW'. Eventually towards the end of the summer, she

119

returned to England.

The Marchioness Anne Queensbury came to stay in the village with her children, and we all became friends. I was attracted to Anne—as was Peter. Such a classy lady who (unfortunately, for her and the children), was separated from her husband, due to his infidelity. We had pleasant social gatherings, and I became fond of the children – Alice, Emma and Torr.

I invited Rosie to visit me and she arrived with her sister and sister's boyfriend. I was really looking forward to seeing Rosie again, as I hadn't been with a woman for several months now—and was feeling decidedly 'horny'.

To my dismay she said she was now having a relationship with Roger, and Roger wouldn't like it if she slept with me. Still, her visit was pleasant and we had some fun together. We had a party before they left, at Anne's house, on the roof terrace. Kerry and Ruth provided live music, to go with the food and wine. Unfortunately, I drank too much and was sick come midnight.

When the house was complete, instead of returning to London, I once again got the crazy idea of travelling around the world—*unbelievable*. I had clearly not learned the lesson from the *'Round The World'* abortive trip to Paris with Brian.

A girl called Barbie Campbell-Cole (another debutant) who had been introduced to our group by Kerry—I think he had designs on her, but without success—expressed an interest in joining me for the journey, at least as far as Spain. We set off in her Mini and spent a couple of weeks driving down to the Spanish border. There was nothing between us before we started the journey, not even a kiss, but stopping at a hotel at the end of the first day, we discovered our room only had a double bed. We agreed to make do.

She spoke fluent French and had dealt with the booking, so maybe it wasn't a surprise to her . . . She was a very attractive, blonde woman—so what the heck. When the inevitable fun started, I asked about contraception and she said,

"It's ok, I have my cap in".
I said,

"I thought this wasn't planned?"
She said,

"It was just a precaution, in case something happened. "

Well, something did happen—and subsequently, happened at every opportunity we could find, over the next two weeks—at last, my sanity was saved.

We had a spooky experience at one of the guesthouses we spent a couple of nights in, close to the Spanish border—there was a bathroom with a separate, adjacent toilet. The proprietress had a mature son—too mature to be still living with his mum . . . The bathroom had a false ceiling with a skylight—ostensibly, for borrowed light. It had been painted out for privacy, but some paint had been scratched away. In the adjacent toilet, was placed a step ladder—innocently it first seemed, but when Barbie was taking a bath on the first night, she saw to her horror, a face looking down on her. It was the son.

To check this out, I relocated the ladder elsewhere, but it immediately reappeared. Barbie, then went into the bathroom again and sure enough, I heard the son leave his room, go into the toilet and I could hear him climbing the stepladder. He was using it as access to the ceiling window.

Echoes of actor Anthony Perkins in Psycho's 'Bates Motel'. Barbie and I deliberated on whether his mother knew, or not—should we say something? She was such a sweet old woman, but we figured whether she knew or not, we couldn't say anything—we left, post-haste.

This bizarre situation aside, we had a pleasant time together and I succeeded in more than making up for enduring the previous year without any sexual encounters. The weather wasn't great at this time of year, so no sunbathing or swimming—anyway we'd both had enough sun by this time. I was doing a lot of reading in those days and we spent our time discussing books, walking, and visiting historical sites—Carcassonne was one of the more spectacular locations we visited.

Eventually, she dropped me at the Spanish border—

she had wanted to accompany me into Spain but had (previously), lost her Passport. On the drive down, we had tried without success, to get a replacement at the British Embassy, in Marseille. Once in Spain, I hitched down the coastal route as far as Barcelona. I found a nice cheap 'pension' and went out to eat and explore the city. I found myself in Las Ramblas, very beautiful tree-lined boulevard, absolutely full of people taking the evening air. Visiting a couple of bars for a drink, I was taken aback by the women who seemed to be admiring me . . . it was only sometime later that I discovered Las Ramblas was where all the local prostitutes plied their trade.

After a couple of days, I cut inland to Madrid. One lift was with a guy in an open top car, which was pleasant, but every half-an-hour or so, he would dowse himself from a bottle of cologne and say,

"Para el refrigerio."

I was slightly concerned he might be gay and trying to make a pass at me. Anyway, I arrived in Madrid okay. After spending a few days there, I boarded a train to Malaga. The train was amazing—light years ahead of anything in the UK at the time. It had double-glazed windows with venetian blinds in-between and was air-conditioned. Arriving in Malaga was quite a shock to step off the train into the fierce heat. Never experienced before, and since, except after a long flight to some tropical country. I then hitched down to Gibraltar, and when I arrived at the border checkpoint, I was directed by a British 'bobby' to the TocH hostel. This was a great place, managed by a nice guy.

After enjoying Gibraltar for a few days—it's such a strange mix, with the Bobbies, red telephone booths, marching bands and typical British pubs—then it was across to North Africa.

Staying in Algiers, along with a fellow traveller I met at TocH, I had my first 'Joint'. We had no choice—this local drug dealer followed us everywhere—he would even come and sit at our table when we had a restaurant meal. Eventually, we gave in and bought his offerings. After dark, we went down to the beach and smoked the joints—it was good stuff. Eventually, I made my—unsteady—way back to the Youth Hostel where we were staying. Laying on my bed, alone in the dark, listening to Arabic singing on a distant radio, I was convinced I understood every word.

The dormitory we were sleeping in was bedbug free—everywhere you went in Tangiers, every single hotel had a sign hanging outside, claiming to be bedbug-free, so we considered ourselves lucky. Unfortunately, after the second night there, we were awoken late at night by the hostel manager. He told us we had to move into a different dormitory. It seems a coachload of German tourists had just arrived and they were to be given our dormitory.

Past Tense

Why became clear later—we were a disparate group, lacking the clout of a German tour group, and our new dormitory was completely infested with bedbugs. Nothing could be done to keep them at bay—removing the mattress and sleeping on the bedsprings, did not help one jot. Their favourite trick was to scuttle across the ceiling and then, with unnerving accuracy—drop down onto you, as you cringed in your sleeping bag.

There was blood—everywhere.

Eventually, we could bear it no longer, and all moved into the hostel reception area and spent the night trying to sleep, sitting upright. The hostel manager thought this very funny—making a pincer gesture with thumb and finger and saying,

"Nip, nippy, nip."

The next day, after having lunch in the Place Petit Socco, a couple of us strolled to the beach. Minutes after we left, the police raided the café and rounded up all the Westerners suspected of using drugs, ready for deportation the next day.

Close shave . . . but as it happens, we left on the same boat as the deportees. Back in the TocH hostel, we had to undergo the usual debugging routine. TocH was a great place to stay—but it was located right against the lower fortifications. The monkeys would come down the walls and into the hostel courtyard. You had to watch out for them—they would steal anything.

One evening, a group of us went for a meal in a local

café. I had a delicious Spanish omelette. There was a Jukebox and, to my delight, on it I found a (new to me, not having heard a radio for a year), Beatles single— 'Paper Back Writer', with 'Rain' on the B-side—it was played all evening.

I then realised I was going to need some more money soon and decided to phone Barbie in London. For some reason, you could not phone London direct from a phone booth in Gibraltar, so I had to cross back into Spain and go to the main Post Office in 'La Linea'. Being unable to make the call at the time, due to opening time restrictions, I returned to Gibraltar. On my return to Spain later in the day, knowing I had to have a minimum amount of money before I would be allowed back into Gibraltar, I borrowed some from my travelling companion, leaving him my watch as security. On my subsequent return to Gibraltar, I was dismayed to find you were not allowed to use the same border crossing, twice on the same day.

So now, I had to travel all around the bay to Algeciras and catch the ferry across the bay, entering Gibraltar via the sea border point. This took all day and my companion was somewhat concerned I had run off with his money.

With the little money I had borrowed, I then set off to hitchhike my way back to London. On the way back up through Spain, I decided to take a detour into Portugal. This I undertook by local bus. All luggage, including my rucksack and banjo, went up on the roof of the bus, along with chickens and the odd goat or two. Once all the seats were occupied, then other seats were folded down into the aisle. We were sitting five abreast, with no way of moving from your seat. I tried not to think about the chaos that would ensue, in the event of an accident.

Happily, I arrived safely in Lisbon, which I found to be a beautiful city. I spent a few days there, sightseeing, visiting the old town and the Castle, with the pink Flamingos residing inside. The view of the bridge, from my 'Pension' window, was striking—it looks just like the San Francisco, Golden Gate bridge. I was surprised by the number of police around the city, armed with automatic rifles—this was a result of the troubles in the Portuguese African colonies. I was drawn into a conversation with an English-speaking local, who insisted that I could not be English. On showing him my passport, he said,

"That means nothing; I could have one of those."
He was friendly enough though. I then resumed my journey home and made my way north, again, up through Spain, towards the French border.
A day or two after entering France, towards the end of the day, I stopped as it was beginning to grow dark. I was exhausted from walking (mostly in the rain) and my feet were so wet—I was getting 'Trench Foot'. I

needed to find somewhere to sleep. The rain had stopped, and bedding down in woodland to the side of the road, I quickly fell into a deep sleep. In the middle of the night, I was awoken by torrential rain—it was so heavy, I could hardly breathe from the shock of it. Packing my belongings as quickly as possible, I set off into the night. After blundering through the woods for a while, I eventually came across a farm and entered an open barn, in which was a very old pickup truck. It had a bench seat, so leaving my rucksack outside, I stretched out on the seat and quickly fell asleep again.

About four o'clock in the morning, the driver's door was wrenched open, and there was the farmer standing menacingly above me—I babbled on to him about,

"La Pluie, pardon Monsieur, la pluie."

"Oui" he replied.

"Aller, aller maintenan."

I scrambled out of the cab and set off again into the darkness. I eventually found a bus stop with a bench and canopy and managed to doze there for a while, until the morning workers started to gather for the bus to their place of work. Off I had to tramp again.

Having spent a year in the sun, I was very brown. Consequently, I attracted a lot of attention from motorbike riding, Gendarmes. They would frequently stop and demand to see my Papers. Even now, back in England, people often refuse to believe I am English.

I eventually ran out of money and, threw myself at the mercy of the British Embassy in Bordeaux. I discovered they don't just hand out a train ticket and wish you a pleasant trip—I was sent to spend three nights in an 'Institut de Nuit', while waiting for money to arrive from my friend Brian, in London. The first time you entered the Institut, you had to strip naked, and while you were being hosed down by one guy, another was closely, *very closely* inspecting your underwear. Then came the delousing powder into your hair.

Five o'clock in the morning and you were given bread and a bowl of soup and then thrown out into the street again. Those three days were exhausting—I was so tired, I just wanted to sleep all the time. I had no money, nothing to do and nowhere to go, except the local park, where I would sleep on a bench until a Gendarme prodded me with his stick and made me move on. Eventually, the embassy gave up waiting for the money and (on my third, daily visit), they gave me a train ticket back to London.

For a while, it was strange being back in London. The different architecture, the hustle and bustle—and the girls were all so pale skinned. I was so used to seeing beautiful bronzed bodies everywhere (usually naked on the nudist beach) and now the complete contrast of these pale creatures, seemed most attractive.

Ramatuelle, Var, France

Peter Crofton-Sleigh was also back in London, and he put some work my way. I spent a few months doing building and decorating, fitted kitchens and stuff like that. I was staying with some Bradford college people, who graduated a year or two behind me. They had a huge flat in St Johns Wood, just up from the tube station. It was located above a solicitor's office and after office hours, we could make as much noise as we liked. Rosie was now living there with Roger and they were to be married . . . One evening, in the kitchen, he confided in me that he thought Rosie was too good for him. Damn right, I thought. He went on to treat her badly and after she had born two children, he dumped her for another woman.

I met up with Barbie again to repay the money I had borrowed while in Gibraltar, and we (of course) dated for a while. She had just bought a new flat in South Kensington and I helped her fixing up shelves and other DIY tasks. I soon realised that, outside the holiday romance scenario, we were just too different. It was great sleeping with her, but it could not last. We agreed to remain friends.

Meanwhile, along with a John Bunce and Dave Cockshott, who also lived in the flat, I was doing odd bits of freelance design work—so we converted the main living-room into a studio. We had some terrific parties there during which, I encountered various women, and had a great time.

Bentley/Farrell/Burnett

It was after Peter Bentley came back from Canada, I had my first LSD trip—actually, it was only a quarter of a trip. It was a Saturday night, Peter and I were at Brian and Dot's flat, getting ready to go to a party. I don't recall where it came from, but we had a single LSD trip in the form of a sugar cube. We dissolved the cube in a cup of water and then shared it out equally, into four small glasses.

I was sitting on the sofa, reading a book and complaining that nothing seemed to be happening when suddenly, I said,

"Oh, oh!"

The words on the page were starting to do funny things. Peter laughed aloud, joined by the others. Off we went to the party and had a wonderful time. I felt fantastic—we all did. Being only a quarter of a trip, nothing too extreme happened—just a tremendous sense of wellbeing, coupled with friends, music and alcohol. Peter had brought back a Racoon coat from Canada, which I borrowed for the evening—it felt great wearing it.

The four of us then started having regular, full trips together, in Brian and Dot's flat. We would have good music to listen to, along with nice food and drink. The music of choice was (of course), The Beatles Sargent Pepper album. This was a safe, controlled environment to experiment with LSD. A trip would (more or less), take care of the weekend and we would be ready for work again, on Monday.

One Sunday morning, Peter and I, had our first outdoors LSD trip together, in Hyde Park. This seemed quite brave at the time. It was a lovely sunny day and there was a brass band playing on the bandstand, with people in deck chairs, all around. We spent all day in the park, helping each other to keep things under control, and then in the evening, found a nearby pub for food and drink.

I first met Dick Negus of Negus & Sharland, during this period. Peter worked there and recommended me to Dick, to help out with a major exhibition they were doing the graphics and display for. I found Dick to be a bit of a letch—the first time I met him to be briefed on the work, he was jogging my elbow and pointing at a girl behind us Julie. Bending over her desk, she was exposing the tops of her stocking and suspenders. I was very embarrassed. On the one hand, I was in awe of this big-name designer, but on the other, rather shocked. I was to discover later that the Negus & Sharland practice was to end—it seems Dick had been sleeping with Philip Sharland's wife. I met her, and she was an attractive woman.

I was handing out pieces of work to the whole graphics team, including (stocking-tops) Julie. She would come and stand by my desk, looking like a love-sick puppy—even when I had no work to give her. Eventually, I dated her a couple of times, but nothing sexual.

It was the largest exhibition I have ever worked on, and prior to the opening of the exhibition, I worked for three days without sleep. Then I crawled off to bed feeling ill and missed the end-of-project party I had been so looking forward to.

As nothing much else was happening workwise, for either of us—I suggested to Peter that we head off down to Ramatuelle for the summer. Barbie was also returning there, so we drove down in her mini. She was working as a 'Peanut Girl' in St Tropez—walking around wearing a mini skirt and sparkling makeup calling,

"Cacahuète, Cacahuète."

Peter and I would sometimes hide when we saw her coming. As much as I would have enjoyed sex, I didn't sleep with her while we were there. It was difficult with Peter sharing the same room.

We spent three months there and had a terrific time. We bought new Solex Bicycles in St Tropez (so much better than my old one), and we zoomed around all over the place. Once on our way to visit Norman—a friend of mine who lived in a ruined village up in the hills, behind St Maxime, we were tearing along a dirt logging trail through the wooded hills when, rounding a bend, we were suddenly confronted with the wonderful French actress Jean Moreau in the middle of the track. I almost ran her down. Such a beautiful woman. I was speechless.

Norman was a great character. He was the only person living in this village, in a house he had restored. The hills around this area and much of France, are riddled with deserted and ruined villages—the result of a whole generation of men, lost in the two world wars. Even Ramatuelle was missing that war generation— there was just one guy of that age—he wasn't very nice. I think he was generally regarded with suspicion by the village . . . why was he still alive? I think it might have been him who put the customs onto Peter Crofton-Sleigh about his telescope.

Peter and I often visited Norman, unfortunately, we never encountered Jean Moreau again. Our daily routine was to rise late, shower and then stroll out to the Café de l'Ormeau on the village square for breakfast. Croissants avec au beurre et confiture, et un grande café au lait. Then it was down to Madame Arnaux's shop to buy a big bag of fruit, before heading off to the beach. We always went to L'Escalet, which was a mixture of white sand and sparkling rocks—it was also the nudist beach. We would spend all day there—trying not to get an erection—and then return to the village for a glass or two of chilled rose, at l'Ormeau.

Bastille Day in St Tropez was amazing—every bar you went in, was serving free beer. There were music and dancing in the Place de Lice, and a good time was had by all. We joined up with a group of people, including an American woman and a gay guy who was staying with her. After midnight, we went skinny dippy on Pampelonne beach.

Somewhere around here, I became separated from Peter, and then found myself in the back of the American woman's VW Beetle, on the way up into the hills behind St Maxime. I was sandwiched—tightly—between one of the women and the gay guy . . . quite an interesting ride. Now, I was stuck up in the hills, waiting for the owner of the car—and the house we were guests in—to drive me back to Ramatuelle. I confirm that nothing untoward happened between the gay guy and myself, but his constant attention was somewhat irksome.

I was pleased to see the Marchioness Anne Queensbury and the children Alice, Emma and Torr, arrive in the village again, widening our social circle beyond just the two of us.

Peter and I then met Angie—an attractive America woman who was staying in the village. She too had a Solex and so one evening, the three of us rode up the hill to Gassin, for food and drinks. The conversation eventually got onto drugs and LSD in particular.

When we mentioned we had been taking regular trips in London, she said,

> "Oh, I've got some LSD back in my room. I've had
> them a long time, but it's probably still okay."

We all jumped on our Solex and zoomed down the hills, back to the village. In a drawer were three pieces of blotting paper . . . This turned out to be the strongest trip I ever experienced.

I had heard about the 'Out-of-body-experience, 'Death and rebirth' etc., but this was the only time I can truly say, I experienced it myself. At one point I found myself floating on the ceiling, looking down at Peter and Angie huddled over a small cassette player on the bed. We listened to 'Sargent Pepper's lonely hearts Club Band'—all night long. In the morning we went out for a walk in the olive groves around the village, observing the (seemingly), giant Crickets and other strange and wonderful creatures.

Back in the village, Kerry collared me.

> "Can you take photos of these paintings, while I
> hold them against this stone wall?"

Past Tense

I focused the camera on a painting but I was completely incapable of actually pressing the shutter release . . . .

"Okay." He said. "Take the photo, take the photo. Take the photo now!"

After what seemed like an eternity and only two paintings down, I had to confess my predicament. Peter and I had a nice (platonic), time with Angie, but eventually, she had to return to her job in Paris, and by this time we were running out of money.

We sold our Solex to a local villager for train fare and returned to London. There, we moved back into the St Johns Wood flat, on a temporary basis.

Chrissie, who I had still not managed to get to grips with—so to speak, was now living in one of the rooms. I really did like her. I attended a college ball, where she was doing a teacher's training course and she jumped on me, like a drowning woman. Dave 'Cocky' Cockshott (as his nickname suggests), was sexually rabid, if it moved, he would screw it—if I am honest I was somewhat the same. Anyway, he was pissed at me turning up and ruining his carefully laid plans, to seduce Chrissie.

Back at the flat, she and I spent the night together but (as it turned out), it was the wrong time of the month . . . . She then disappeared over the horizon—it seemed she had a boyfriend—and so I took over her room. I found a diary she had left in a drawer. In it, she had written,

"I don't know what it is about Bunny. He just
doesn't have enough oomph."

Well, thank you . . . .

Never the less, she did visit me a couple of times later
and we did—*finally*—have sex in her old (now my)
room. I think she was trying to understand what she
wanted—because sometime later she married her boyfriend, and I was the wedding photographer—I'm
happy to say—I put the film into the camera
sprocket—correctly, this time.

I was now sharing the flat with Roger, Rosie, John
and Dave (Cocky), Cockshott. This was when I first
met Stephanie. Ron, one of the Bradford College tutors,
came down to London for the weekend, bringing along
some of his students—one of whom was Stephanie.
We were drinking in the St Johns Wood tube station
bar (it was the nearest pub), and Ron asked me to meet
her at the top of the escalator. She came off the escalator towards me, and there was immediate chemistry.
Turns out, she was supposed to be having a naughty
weekend with Ron.

Later that evening, after we had all downed several pints and were back at the flat, I was in the living
room, chatting to one of the other females in Ron's
party—she was sitting at my feet, looking up at me . . .
It was evident we were going to end up in my room
and in my bed. Then, Stephanie enters 'stage left' and

demands the female spends the night with her, in the spare room. I don't know whether she just didn't want to sleep with Ron (although, I think she had previously slept with him), or whether she had already set her sights on me and didn't want to 'mucky her ticket' so to speak? There was certainly enough chemistry between us.

Now, we males are all in the kitchen, consoling each other, wondering what had just happened.

"Stupid women." Ron said.

"Yeah, it beats me, I was set up there." I said.

Dot, Peter and I were now living in a terrific two-floor flat above a United Dairies shop in Crouch End, right by the clock tower. Sometimes I would lie awake at night listening to the double-clunk sound of people getting cartons of milk from the vending machine, immediately below my feet.

Dot had separated from Brian with whom she had had a child, and he was living there with us. It was a great social period, with frequent evenings spent in the Queens pub. The Hornsey Art College was still based in Crouch End, and the students had adopted the Queens as their local. There was a DJ every night and we had some great times in there. It was in the Queens that I first met my wife to be—Kate. We slept together once, but it didn't go anywhere at the time. She used to occasionally baby-sit for Peter and Dot, which could be a bit awkward, as she might be baby-sitting in the adjacent bedroom on the occasions I returned with some lady or other, to spend the night with. Kate remained on the periphery of our crowd, but we never really got together again during this period.

Dot, had studied fashion at Bradford, and decided to start up her own fashion boutique. Peter and I were asked to provide the design scheme for the branding and boutique interior. So, we started the 'Bentley/Burnett Design' practice, 'Bosies' being our first project. The boutique was in the Saville row area. It was trendy and upset a lot of Saville Row suit-wearing gentlemen.

Vanessa, an ex-flatmate of Patsy, was running a courier service around town. Initially, she used her MGB sports car but changed it for a more practical Minivan—she was collecting all the dresses for the boutique from the 'Outworkers'. We eventually started a relationship. which lasted for a while and the sex was good.

At a party one night, we were dancing together and things got a little steamy—she said,

"Come with me."

She lead me by the hand, down into the street, where her Minivan was parked. Into the back we went—not very comfortable, but satisfying. Afterwards, we returned to the party, as if nothing had happened. I hope the van wasn't rocking too much.

Peter and I then joined up with a former work colleague of Peter's (Michael Farrell), who I also had met previously, and so we became *'Bentley/Farrell/Burnett'*. Michael had a studio in London mews, Paddington, and was looking for a partner to replace one who had left. So, it worked out very well for all of us.

Peter and Michael were both graphic designers and the majority of the work they did, was book jacket design, for virtually all the London publishing houses. They did some successful series of book jackets for Penguin Books, for example, all the Evelyn Waugh novels, Raymond Chandler's novels and many others.

We were fortunate to have our work published in many of the main design publications, in England and around the world. We had quite a collection of DADA Awards and stubby, yellow pencils. There would be an annual awards night dinner—a bit like the BAFTAs. One was held at the Park Lane Hilton and another at the Royal College of Art—at which, the prizes were presented by a Ken Campbell and his robot. These events were always great fun but invariably ended with us all being very drunk.

It lasted nearly 4 years and we had a terrific time, this was—after all—the swinging sixties.

I had a couple of trips, at the St Johns Wood flat. One was after Chrissie's wedding—I'd hit it off with one of the female guests and as we were having a party, I invited her back to the flat afterwards. A few of us had taken LSD, so (after due consideration), I told the girl it would be better to meet again another day.

We did meet, but nothing came of it. The party was a bit wild, with some people, not dealing with their trip well. This reaffirmed my belief that you have to use LSD in a controlled environment, with people you trusted.

The other was one Bank holiday weekend. Everyone had gone back up North and I had the whole flat to myself. I was actually meant to be seeing a woman I'd met at one of our parties and slept with, but I didn't really want to. Early Saturday evening, having taken the trip, I was sat in the living room, feeling the initial tingling sensations and listening to Hendricks 'Purple Haze'. The music generated such strong sensual feelings; I quite regretted not being with a woman. When it got late, I remember watching the old black and white film 'Twelve O'clock High', with Gregory Peck and Dean Jagger.

As a result of wet shaving, I developed a rash on my face. It would not go away. I went to the doctor and he gave me a cortizone cream. This worked a treat but, after a while, my moustache turned blond and eventually, started to disappear. After some time, I realised I no longer needed to shave—hair was no longer growing on my face.

At first, I thought, this is great—I no longer have the chore of shaving every day. But then I began to worry that it might spread to my hair—*not so good*.

For a little while, I was dating (Julia) the girl I met at

142

Past Tense

Dick Negus' office. Her parents lived on Hayling Island and one hot summer weekend, we went down there when her parents were away. We had an afternoon sailing in her father's dinghy and lots of sunbathing. We were sunbathing naked in the garden when, to our surprise, her elder sister turned up with her boyfriend. After rapidly dressing, we joined them in the conservatory for refreshments. It turned out that the boyfriend was a doctor. Though not so old, he was trying to look the part by smoking a bent pipe—*plonker*.

Julia then embarrassed me by relating my rash problem to him. I explained the situation and expressed my concern it would spread to my hair.

"Oh no," he says, puffing on his pipe.

"That won't happen'.

He was wrong of course —It did.

When we returned to London on Sunday evening, we were both so sunburnt, we could not bear to have sex. We both just laid there with no sheet touching our inflamed skin.

BFB did various exhibition projects for the GPO and, after one, we were all lined up for inspection and introduction, to the then Postmaster General—the late Anthony Wedgewood Benn. He was such a strikingly handsome man.

Along with Peter and Dot, Michael (now separated from his wife) and I, decided to go to Ramatuelle, for a holiday. We booked the house I had renovated, but then Peter and Dot decided they could not afford to go, so Michael and I flew off to Nice alone. After a while, two of Michaels's friends joined us. They had driven down in the ubiquitous mini—it seemed like absolutely everybody drove a Mini in those days. They brought a record player and LPs with them—this was how I discovered Joni Mitchell. We listened to her, constantly throughout the holiday.

One of the restored properties backing onto our rear terrace had a party and invited us all across. It was a high-class affair, with a whole pig, roasting on a spit, over a huge, open fire. Seemed a bit inappropriate to me, given the heat, at the time of year, but it was great fun. All too soon the holiday came to an end, and we returned to London.

Ray Newell was a graphic designer, who did some free-lance for us. Ray and his wife Wendy lived in Putney. Apart from being a designer, Ray also ran a mobile disco for private parties. They were great fun and we went to many parties with them—we were sort of a 'rent-a-crowd', to make up party numbers.

They had a party at their flat one Friday evening and I turned up with an envelope full of grass I had received that day—a friend-of-a-friend used to turn up at the studio on Fridays with this surprisingly cheap, South African grass. I kept rolling a joint for one friend or another but—on losing sight of them—would end up smoking it myself. Combined with a goodly supply of alcohol, this resulted in me finding myself in the front garden under a bush—being sick—I thought I might die. It's easy to understand when reading of 'Rock Stars' dying, by choking on their own vomit. Horrible. Over the course of several parties, Wendy made it clear that she was keen on me and we eventually arranged to meet secretly. She was attractive and sexy and I could not bring myself to refuse her advances. We had lunchtime drinks together at the Atlas pub, in Seagrave Road. On the next assignation, we went to the cinema together and then back to her flat. Ray was away in the country, and Wendy was going to join him the next day.

We had a great night of sex together then, and on future occasions—the design studio floor being a memorable one. Eventually, she withheld sexual privileges from Ray and of course, he immediately knew something was up. She confessed to Ray, and so I decided it was best to end it. I don't know if she confessed whom she was having the affair with, because, sometime later, I met them both at a Royal College party—Ray did not punch me in the face, so perhaps not. Anyway, I was glad to see they were still together, in spite of my intrusion.

Stephanie had now moved to London, and (despite my initial protestations), was now living with me in the Crouch End flat I shared with Peter and Dot.

Stephanie and I took our first LSD together here. We walked along Park Road, up through Queens Wood and into Highgate Woods and playing fields. It was quite a challenge to do this in the woods, with the trees, leaves, insects, birds—nature assaulting our senses. It was difficult to look in any one direction for more than a few seconds before everything started to become alive and overwhelming.

While BFB seemed to have plenty of work, book jackets did not bring in enough money—twenty-one guineas for the design and artwork—that is £22.05p, in today's money. Exhibitions when I got them, brought in much more money.

We were gradually going broke and, along with Michael's marital problems, the situation was not looking good. After consulting a business advisor, we closed the practice and went our separate ways. I spent the next year doing bits of free-lance, designing and building, Air-supported-structures and an air-driven, toy train with an ex-client and now friend, the late Angus Wallace.

After some failed attempts at working with other designers, Peter Disappeared off to Wales, I think to be a carpenter and last I heard, he was living on some Greek Island, doing what exactly, I have no idea—probably not design. Michael emigrated and went to Australia with design colleagues and formed a successful design practice there. He ended up working alone and, as I only recently discovered, an accidental fall resulted in a brain haemorrhage, plunging him into a coma for a year. Just when the doctors were about to switch off his life support—he suddenly woke up. Being wheelchair bound and unable to work, he returned to England for a while but then went back to Australia. Sadly, after an epileptic fit, he died in 1996.

Air City

A ngus and I had a company called Air City Limited. We designed an indoor air-supported structure for the Advertising Associations Conference and exhibition in Brighton, and an outdoor, reusable Discothèque for the Kent Messenger newspaper; its first appearance being at a race meeting at Brands Hatch. The Brighton project was quite eventful. Initially, we were staying in the Grand Hotel, but given one of the installation crew was, to say the least, a bit hippy-ish, with long hair, leather jacket complete with chains, and in the habit of walking through reception barefoot—after a couple of days we were (politely), asked to leave.

So then we were moved into the Queens. Where we lasted for a few days, but then out we had to go. For the remainder of the project, we ended up in a borrowed flat in Hove. The structure was manufactured in Holland, so Angus, his family and I, went to Amsterdam to meet the people who made it. Angus was driving an old Mercedes-Benz hearse, at the time, and we travelled in that. The children and I were laid out in the back, like recently deceased. We stayed with the guys who were making the inflatable, in their house by the side of a canal, outside Amsterdam. They were real hippy types and we had some fun, while we were there. I remember 'window shopping' in the red-light district. Most of the prostitutes seemed to be Indonesian—from the Dutch colonial days—and were all very beautiful. I reiterate, I just window-shopped.

We went to an art festival in a park filled with amazing air-supported structures. We were excited about this new concept for buildings. It seemed like the future to us.

The Brands Hatch project was fun. We teamed up with the son of a factory owner, who manufactured TIR lorry tarpaulins. They agreed to provide all the material for us to manufacture the disco ourselves, in their factory.

The son obviously liked being part of our scene, but he was a bit crazy—especially when he got behind the wheel of his sports car. Whenever we were to travel anywhere, there was a desperate scramble, *not to be the one* who had to ride with him—terrifying.

Angus now had a 1949 Bentley, a beautiful old car that I loved driving. Angus seemed content to allow me to act as chauffeur. A much safer mode of transport. I don't know how Angus managed to have a seemingly endless procession of old cars. Inflatable structures never really took off in the UK. They are used for Warehousing, but nothing exciting.

Our windowless office-workshop, was located deep in the bowels of Kentish Town tube station. We had to walk through a print shop storeroom, to get to our door, and then down into the depths.

We were now designing an air-driven, toy train set. We tried selling it to the big toy manufacturers, without success. We took it to Triang and the person we met there said,

"Have you managed to get it to hover vertically?"

"Yes", I said.

"Oh," he said,

"That explains why we've been having all these power cuts."

The cost of making the prototype train had been covered by a friend of Angus'. He was a rich gynaecologist, who made his money providing abortions for non-UK residents. The law required women to be resident in the UK for a couple of days before they could have an abortion. The clinic was near Elstree and he bought a local country-side hotel, in which the women could stay, for the mandatory period. It was a lovely old building, with extensive grounds. There were no architects drawings for the hotel, so Angus and I had to do a complete survey. The weather was lovely, so it was a pleasant task. The hotel had a nice bar frequented by the locals. There was some disquiet among the locals about all these women coming for abortions, so the gynaecologist decided to organise a BBQ and party for all the locals. Angus and I rigged up coloured, flood lighting throughout the extensive grounds and it looked impressive. I don't know if it pacified the locals.

Angus and I then drove up to Leeds in the Bentley, to show the train to 'Fisher Price' toys. The gynaecologist had his own aeroplane and flew up to meet us there. After our presentation, Fisher-Price said the train did not have enough 'Play Power'—that was the end of that.

July 20, 1969, Apollo 11 and the Moon landing. I was watching from my sick bed, as I had Flu. I was sat up in bed, surrounded by a Birthday present from Stephanie—the plastic components for a large, scale model of the Saturn 5, Apollo 11 and it was about fifty percent complete. Later, when I went to America, I gave the finished model to Angus' children. By now, the relationship with Pete and Dot had become somewhat strained, so Stephanie and I moved to a flat, in Fulham. The flat was so nice— the nicest I had lived in so far. Stephanie and I decorated it from scratch and everything was, as we would wish it.

As soon as the decorations were finished, I bought my

first stereo system. It was delivered on a Saturday morning and we played it all day and much of the night—our landlord and his wife, came up after dinner, bringing The Who's, 'Tommy' album. It blew us away, and we rushed out and bought it first thing Monday morning.

We had some nice times there. Friends visiting, parties, and just listening to music.

Every Saturday morning I would go to the local florist and buy a big bunch of Freesias—you had to get there in good time before wedding events took them all. The scent was so delicious and seemed to permeate the flat. Smelling freesias now always reminds me of times spent in the flat. It is still a happy smell. I learnt to drive there, and when I passed the test, Angus loaned me an old Renault 4L. It was tomato red and the bonnet had psychedelic flames all over the bonnet. Unfortunately, there was no ignition key and one had to start it by reaching under the dashboard and rubbing the appropriate wires together.

This was okay when starting out on a journey, but it also had a tendency to overheat, to the extent that, in heavy town traffic, it would just stop. Typically, this would happen at the most inopportune times—top of Tottenham Court Road, for example.

I was bending over, head resting on the steering wheel, trying to find and connect the appropriate wires when there was a woman knocking on the side window,

Past Tense

"Are you alright?" she asked.

What could I say? Every time this happened, I was afraid someone would think I was either suffering a heart attack or had stolen the car and was trying to by-pass the ignition. Fortunately, the car started and I zoomed off—as far as the next traffic jam. It turned out the cylinder head was cracked and it was only running on three cylinders. I wasted many hours in the street outside our flat, trying to fix it, to no avail. Even all the knowledge passed to me by Des, couldn't help with this one.

I introduced Stephanie to Jim and Wendy Downer and we started going sailing with them. Jim, now had his own boat—a six berth trimaran. He never took it out of the water, sailing all through the winter. Some weekends, we would join them and it would be so cold and windy, we would spend the weekend in our bunks reading, going for walks when the weather allowed. We also spent a summer holiday with them, sailing around the Solent and the South coast.

One weekend, we spent hours beating (close-hauled down the Solent, against strong winds and seas, until we finally reached Newtown Creek. Gliding into the sheltered calm of the mud banks was such a wonderful contrast to the ferocious weather. My senses were so heightened that the mud banks displayed every colour of the rainbow. I felt so high, like being on LSD—tripping on nature.

Air City

With some design fees I received, I bought a beautiful old Ford Consul, from a guy down the street. It had red bench seats and a steering mounted gearshift. It was white with a black roof and I loved it—spending many hours, out in the street, fussing over it.

One bank holiday weekend, we decided to drive up North to visit family. Off we set, Stephanie and me up front and three friends in the back. After an hour or so, Dave Edwards started complaining there was smoke, making him cough—he was asthmatic, so I didn't think much of it. However, after a while, it became obvious something was not quite right. Stopping at the next service station, I found the oil dipstick lying on top of the engine—I replaced it. Stopping again later, to check what was causing the strange noises and smoke, I again found the oil dip-stick lying on top of the engine—I could have sworn I replaced it—and did so again.

This was repeated several times before we arrived in Pudsey. Saturday morning, Des and I drove to a shed in Stanningley bottom he used as a garage, and started to strip down the engine. Off came the cylinder head and all was revealed—the pistons were burnt through, and the combustion was blowing down through the oil sump and blowing the dipstick out of its housing. Into Leeds City, we went and bought four new pistons. We then spent the whole bank holiday weekend putting the engine back together. It was cold in the shed, and this was the time of the UK power cuts. When the lights went out, we had to walk home in the cold. I didn't see Stephanie or any friends for the whole weekend. Eventually, we drove slowly (to run-in the new pistons), back to London and the Fulham flat.

Stephanie and I decided to go for a holiday to Ramatuelle. I had told her so much about the village; she was longing to see it. We invited Rodney, Angus, Mary and their son Babel, to make up numbers and allow us to afford the rent for the house I had worked on. We were in two cars, the Consul and Angus in some huge American car he'd acquired. After an overnight in Paris, we drove non-stop to the south — snatching some sleep in Service stations. I had bought an Eight-track stereo for the car and the night before we left, Rodney stayed up, virtually all night transferring music from my stereo, onto the cassettes.

We had a good time, but inevitably, there was a falling out, between Angus and me. When our rental finished at the house, Angus and family left for London. We stayed on for another week or so — finding another room in the village. Rodney could not afford to stay long, so after a few days, I drove him to St Raphael to catch the train. Stephanie and I had a pleasant time on our own, but eventually our money ran out and we had to leave. The car dynamo was playing up so I took it a garage in St Tropez, and we hung around on the harbour front until it was fixed. We set off back late afternoon and drove non-stop, back to the ferry at Calais—we could not stop because we had no money for food.

We also had no money for Autoroute tolls, so it was the old Route National, the whole way. We just had enough money for petrol—to make sure, driving from Paris to Calais over those long, rolling hills, I would switch off the engine and coast down each hill, switching the engine on again, at the bottom—with relief, we made it to the ferry.

At Dover, I was terrified the petrol would run out before I could drive off the ferry. Making it to a petrol station, just yards from the ferry, I spent the last £1 we had between us, on petrol. Unbelievable now, but it was enough to get us home to Fulham, London.

Stephanie and I had our second LSD trip together, in the flat. It went well and we had a great time together, just talking and listening to music and of course, making love.

We would play tennis together in Bishop's Park, go for walks along the Thames and sit listening to a brass band playing in Fulham Palace Gardens, by Putney Bridge.

Stephanie was studying Drama, and during her summer break and I suggested she go and visit Kerry and Jan in Cambridge, Boston. Kerry and Jan had lived close to us in Fulham for a while and so Stephanie and Jan had become friends. The summer break ended and

Past Tense

Stephanie decided she did not want to come back to London—she was going to take a 'Year Out'.

I think she was (perhaps), having too good a time, and sleeping with one or two guys. Kerry was concerned she was burning the candle at both ends and was trying to persuade me to come over and join them.

During this period, work became thin on the ground and I was at a bit of a loss, what to do with myself. I too was putting myself about a bit and had slept with a couple of women. After the encouragement and invitations from Kerry, I decided to join Stephanie there.

I had no money, so I sold everything I had—my old Ford Consul car, my bed, chairs, stereo, my prototype design light fittings—everything I couldn't put into storage with friends. I even drove up to Pudsey to leave some stuff with my parents. Angus and Mary organised a terrific farewell party for me at their place, and everybody I knew was there. There was a nice Welsh female friend of Angus' there, and I got lucky that night.

I was due to fly out to Boston, Sunday morning, but I didn't manage to sell the car until Saturday evening. This chap turns up and we start it up—the dynamo had been a bit dodgy for some time, especially at low rev's . . .

"Trouble with the electrics?" he said.

"Oh, I don't think so," I said.

Fortunately, at that moment the warning light went

out. My heart was in my mouth —I needed the money to get on the plane, in the morning.

£100 . . . that will do nicely, thank you.

The old adage— A Rolling Stone Gathers No Moss, had proved itself true. Moreover, was to do so again on future occasions.

Cambridge, Boston

This was only my second flight, the first one being on a BEA Trident to Nice, with Michael. This was on the new BOAC Boeing 747. I was thrilled by the size and modern design of the interior—to me, it was like being inside a spaceship. I spent some time admiring the design detailing of the various fixtures and fittings.

I arrived in Boston with £20 in my pocket and they let me in—long hair and all.

The customs officer, head down, looked at my passport and photograph . . . his head snapped up to look at me—it was a poor photograph, making me look even more of a long-haired 'Hippy' than I actually was. Thankfully, he let me pass.

It turned out there wasn't much work there either, with most design companies being on a four-day week, or reduced staff. After interviews with various companies, I picked up the odd bits of free-lance work, but nothing serious or worthwhile. Stephanie was waiting tables at the 'Spaghetti House Emporium' in Harvard Square. She was making good money in tips and bought me an electric shaver, to help with my rash problem. It's the only time a woman has supported me financially. I could do with some of that now—a nice, rich lady would be just the ticket. I loved Cambridge— it's like Chelsea, London, but ten times better. The bars, the restaurants; we could leave our apartment in Green Street, walk in any direction for five or ten minutes, and encounter a bar or restaurant serving great food.

There were thirteen stereo radio stations to choose from— back in London, my 'Rogers' tuner could only receive stereo on Radio Three-classical, for about two hours a day.

Our local bar on Mass' Avenue had free, live Blues music and it was broadcast on the local radio stations. I loved that bar, it had an enormous open charcoal grill, and I swear I had a steak burger and salad, every day. Except for the days, we had delicious stone-oven baked Pizzas, from just a couple of doors further down.

Life seemed so good there, and I was desperate to stay a while—maybe a couple of years or so, but not forever. I felt London, England was—ultimately—the best place to live, work, and one day raise a family.

It's interesting how the balance of power in relationships changes with circumstances. In Cambridge, I guess Stephanie was calling the shots. She worked hard waiting tables, until late at night and then would sit up even later, smoking cigarettes, to wind down. At times, I felt ignored and slightly left out of everything—like I had no purpose being there. I guess I didn't, really.

Attending a job interview in Boston, I was amazed to discover the receptionist was none other than Anita, my long lost Ramatuelle love. Unfortunately, it turned out she was happily married. Good thing too. It could have been messy otherwise, given I was with Stephanie.

Continuing my search for work, I took the train to New York. A female friend of Kerry's had suggested she could fix me up with some accommodation. She had met this guy on holiday in Jamaica—probably slept with him. I didn't ask—she phoned him and he agreed to put me up for a couple of weeks, in his Brooklyn apartment.

I arrived at Grand Central Station late at night and started walking to the Subway station. This turned out to be painful as (due to the action of the Gulf Stream as it passes up the coast past Boston and New York) the atmosphere is very dry. This generates a great deal of static electricity. Every four steps I took resulted in a painful spark jumping between the metal suitcase handle and the rings on my fingers—I was counting as I walked—one, two, three, four—ouch. This is an extreme phenomenon—in our Cambridge apartment, we had large, copper humidifier, constantly pumping out steam. My hair had a tendency to stand on end—like a cartoon of someone receiving an electric shock, and I would sometimes get nosebleeds. You learnt to touch metal door handles with a gloved hand or a part of your body that was clothed, or suffer a painful shock. It could get bitterly cold and I experienced 'Ice rain' for the first time. Everything—buildings, trees, would be coated with ice. The trees especially, looked beautiful. I commented to Kerry about the number of people with plaster-casts on various limbs, wondering where they went skiing,

"It's not from skiing, it's the ice." He said.

I discovered what he meant—walking through Harvard Square, you had to hold onto anything convenient, otherwise, you slowly slid sideways, across the pavement, and into the gutter.

I spent the next several nights in Brooklyn Heights, sharing a double waterbed with a complete stranger. Kevin was a nice guy and made me feel welcome—his not being gay was a definite help. I had job interviews, but no luck, and no job. I wondered about the city sightseeing. With nothing to do one afternoon, I went to see 'The Poseidon Adventure', at a cinema on Broadway. It was only afterwards, I realised I had been on Broadway and Times Square, for that matter. These famous locations did not seem to have the same presence as say, Piccadilly Circus or Trafalgar Square. It was still exciting though, especially the architecture, and I soon got a pain in the neck, from looking upwards. I, of course visited the twin towers and took a great many photographs around Manhattan. Kevin went away for a few days, and Stephanie joined me there. We had a pleasant few days exploring New York. I enjoyed walking up to Brooklyn Heights—the view from there, across to Manhattan was breathtaking. Norman Mailer had a house there, and I took many photographs.

The friendliness of New Yorkers took me by surprise. I had the mistaken impression from media and friends in London, that if you asked someone in the street for the time of day, they would—likely as not—pull out a gun and shoot you.

A similar misconception of America was everything was frantic, with traffic zooming around like crazy everywhere. Not at all true—just the opposite, the huge cars, seemed to waft around, at what to me was a sedate pace.

Back in Cambridge, Kerry was recording an album, using the Orson Wells Film School sound studio, on Mass' Avenue. I would sometimes spend evenings up there, watching and listening. Stephanie and I kept extending our Tourist visas until finally—we had to think about moving.

Cambridge, Boston

Also, we had fallen out with Kerry and Jan and we were now living with two other friends—Gordon and Cindy, in Boston. Cindy was amazing—a gorgeous, real-life, living breathing, Cindy doll—the type you could only find in America. Gordon was outgoing, a talented singer and guitar player and could perform every single Carol King track, with skill.

The brief period we stayed with them, was a bit awkward as we were all sleeping in the same room. Gordon was constantly trying to 'get it on' with Cindy, but she would have none of it,

"No Gordon, stop it, Gordon, don't do that."

until she would end up jumping out of bed, away from him. Meanwhile, I would be trying—discreetly—to 'get it on' with Stephanie, on the other side of the room. She also, was not too keen—our relationship was entering the 'end game' by this time.

My sister May was living in Framingham with her husband Des and two sons (Chris and Phillip), and we were able to stay with them for a couple of weeks over the Christmas period. Framingham is a typical American suburb, with rolling lawns and White, picket fences. It snowed a lot while we were there, and I helped to shovel the driveway clear.

I remember remarking to my sister one day; it seemed so noisy, all the time, in the kitchen. This was because of all the machinery—dishwasher, washing machine, coffee grinder and extractor fans etc. None of which, I had previously experienced, in Pudsey, or indeed London.

We had another friend Luke, who was a White Bahamian. He was returning home to Nassau and invited us to visit him. Gordon's grandparents lived in Fort Lauderdale, so the four of us decided to travel down together, visiting them on the way.

We travelled to Miami by undertaking to deliver a retired couple's car, to Fort Lauderdale. This is a great way of travelling around the states. You phone an Agency, tell them where you want to go and—hopefully—they will have a car for you to deliver. You just have to pay for petrol. When I picked up the car, I was somewhat disappointed to discover that it wasn't a 'Cadillac', just an 'Oldsmobile'. It was still the largest car I had ever driven, and . . . it had 'Air-conditioning'. When we came to open up the boot, to put our luggage in, we found it was completely filled with the owner's luggage—not surprising really. It just hadn't occurred to us.

A quick trip to Walmart was called for, and we purchase a roof rack, on which we strapped the luggage we couldn't get inside the car. We stopped for the night at a motel in Washington. To avoid paying for a room big enough for four people, Stephanie and I hid in the back seats, under all our clothes, while Gordon and Cindy checked in. After a somewhat uncomfortable night, we discovered that we could have had a

Cambridge, Boston

Four-person room, for just another ten US.

Unbelievably, driving down through Carolina, just as we were thinking it would soon be time to turn on the A/C, we were puzzled to see a white dusting of 'something' on the sides of the Freeway. What could it be, we wondered.

Then, quite suddenly we realised what it was. It started to snow—heavily. Visibility was soon reduced to almost zero. I was desperately trying to keep the taillights of the car in front visible, or we would have been in real trouble. I think it was the first snow in 100 years and was declared a 'State Emergency.' Unhappily, several people were trapped on the freeway and died during the night. Running car engines to keep warm in the deep snow, they succumbed to carbon monoxide poisoning. After several attempts, we were lucky to find a motel with an available room.

We were trapped there for three days. Every time we had finished our meal in the motel restaurant, the waitress would smile and say,

"Y'all come back now."

As if we had a choice. Anxiously, I phoned the owners of the car in Fort Lauderdale, but they were expecting our call—the situation was all over the network TV news. Eventually, the snow receded sufficiently, so we could leave. We had to use the waste paper bin from our room, to dig out the car.

We had planned to fit in a visit to the Kennedy Space

Past Tense

Centre, but as we were only allowed three days to deliver the car, and that deadline had long expired—that was now out. We stayed with Gordon's grandparents one night, and then I dropped everybody and the luggage off at Miami Airport. I delivered the car to the owners in Fort Lauderdale and then had to get a couple of buses back to the airport, to join them. It took hours and they thought they had lost me. We took a local flight to Nassau and spent two enjoyable weeks there with Luke—eating Conch fish and drinking Rum and Coke. I thought Nassau was lovely—particularly the old town. But the general landscape was all a bit flat. I was expecting it to be like Jamaica, with dramatic scenery. 'Paradise Beach' was also a big disappointment.

Returning to Miami, Stephanie and I planned to spend the winter there. Gordon and Cindy returned to Boston.

We left our luggage in lockers at the airport, and went into Miami Beach, to search for somewhere to live. We found a nice little house to rent, in the garden of a large house. After we had returned to the airport, collected our luggage and returned to 'our new home', we were tired and hungry. We dropped our luggage in the middle of the living room floor and went out to find food.

We found a welcoming bar, full of friendly people, including some ex-pats. We had burgers, beer and played darts with the locals. We were so happy—the prospect of spending the winter in Miami Beach, in our little house, with a friendly bar just around the corner, was thrilling. When we returned—tired and happy—to the house, we discovered to our horror, we had been robbed of absolutely everything we possessed. I woke the property owner from his bed, demanding he calls the police. He eventually—reluctantly—did so. When the police arrived, they explained his reluctance was because he was a Canadian national and wasn't supposed to rent out property.

The owner had thrown out the previous tenant because he didn't pay his rent. The police said they knew him—he was a local drug addict, but said by the time they would find him, he would have sold everything, to pay for drugs.

Everything was gone, my entire work portfolio, carousel projector, camera and the many rolls of exposed film, taken around Cambridge, Boston and New York. All my work portfolio and exposed films were (of course), worthless to him and would have been thrown in the nearest bin. We were literally left with just the clothes we were stood up in.

To get a job, you first had to get a blood test—this is how you are flagged up as an 'Illegal Alien' in the system. This was in complete contrast to the situation in Cambridge, where Stephanie worked for a year and had a social security number—no problem at all.

The next day, Stephanie got a job in one of the seafront

hotels and actually completed a couple of work shifts. I got a job as a 'short-order-cook', but had not yet started. The next morning, a detective from the A detective from Miami Police arrested us for getting jobs illegally. He put us in his car, where we shared the front bench seat. In the back seat, was an unhappy looking, young Mexican wearing handcuffs.

The officer was very friendly with us, speaking about the time he spent in London during the war, and how much he liked the Brits—he did not handcuff us. At the police station, we were fingerprinted and had our 'Mugshots' taken. We told them the only reason we had tried to get work was the robbery . . . They were able to corroborate this with the local police, so they were sympathetic in their handling of us.

We were told we had to leave America within three months, or be deported. They said we were free to work during the three months, but by this time, we'd both had enough.

I telephoned my sister May in Framingham and she immediately cabled us flight tickets, for London. We left that night. After a year in America, we arrived back at LHR in only the beach clothes we were wearing.

"And how long have you two been in America?" asked the LHR customs officials.

"Oh, a year."

To say they were suspicious is an understatement. However, after a brief explanation, we were allowed on our way.

We threw ourselves at the mercy of Angus and Mary and stayed with them for a while, until Mary started behaving strangely paranoid . . . She became convinced Angus was screwing Stephanie—we would be lying in bed at night, listening to her irrational ravings downstairs. She insisted Angus should tell us to leave, but to his credit, he refused. We clearly could not stay there a minute longer than necessary.

Fortunately, Stephanie found a large double bedsit in Willesden and we were gone. Stephanie was now spending a lot of time, in Bradford, so I was often alone in the bedsit.

Angus threw a great welcome back party for me and I managed to get lucky with Suzie—a girl I'd fancied for a long time. She was sex on a stick and was the ex-girl-friend of Angus' eldest son Darius. He was at the party with his new Dutch girl-friend he'd met while spending some time in Holland. I was having a nice time dancing with another lady I first met in the 'Island Queen' pub, and who I'd admired for some time. Strangely enough, she was also called Susie and it seemed quite likely that we would be spending the night together. Suzie kept pestering me and eventually insisted that I leave the party with her. What a quandary, having to choose between two lovely ladies— both called Susie. I chose Suzie, and we returned to my Willesden bedsit. We had a nice weekend together, but then I never saw her again. By coincidence, Rodney lived just a couple of doors away and he would often come round to play chess with me. And of course, we also resumed our snooker sessions.

London II

I was penniless, so I phoned Richard Negus who (having separated from Philip Sharland), now had the practice—Negus & Negus, located in Royal College Street, Camden Town. The second Negus was his wife Pam. She was not a designer but handled the administration. As luck would have it, they were moving office, and asked me to take care of the project for him—the architect he had on board was not doing a good job. The new location was not a very nice area, but the existing landlord would not renew the lease. I was able to improve the design and reduce the cost of the project, so Dick thought I was the bee's knees. Well, at least for a while anyway.

At the time, they were participating in a limited competition to design the corporate identity for the newly formed national airline 'British Airways.' The other competitors were 'Henrion' and 'Lippincott &

172

Margulies.' I ended up helping them with the three-dimensional aspects of this, and they succeeded in winning the competition, and the extremely lucrative contract. I remember—at short notice—having to load up Pam's Mini with the large aircraft models we had produced in the new livery, and along with a work colleague (Susan), drive like a maniac through London, down to the Hilton Hotel. The press release conference was being held there, and we were both rather nervous assembling the models in front of the whole British Airways board. They were all sitting there, waiting to start. We left the room and the press were admitted.

Dick took the whole studio out for a celebration dinner at a 'Camden Lock' restaurant, followed by a barge cruise up and down the Regents Canal. There was music and more drinks on board, along with the odd joint or two. Having just come back from the Bahamas where I had discovered Bacardi and Coke, I inevitably got drunk and eventually crawled off to find somewhere to die. Mixing alcohol and dope—not a good idea.

I was curled into the foetal position, in the dirt by the canal edge, and concealed from my colleagues by a low wall. I was being sick—again, as in Putney, I thought I was going to die. This did not do my white, tropical suit any good, at all.

Some Bargees found me, and after much discussion and pouring buckets of canal water over me, they threw me in the back of a Mini-van, and dropped me outside my Willesden bed-sit—I don't know how they got an address out of me?

It took me a couple of days to resurface. No phone or mobile then, so I had to crawl to the nearest telephone booth, and let the studio know I was still alive. When I returned to the studio the following day, my colleagues all thought this was very funny . . . Pricilla Purcell-Young, a debutant lady, graphic designer was quite interested in me, and I in her. I think I was the 'boy from the wrong side of the tracks'. I tried one or two subtle advances, but it never came to anything. Her family would never have approved. On my return she said,

"I was worried about you and was going to come and find you if you did show today"

Thank God that didn't happen. I would have died of embarrassment. Anyway, she soon found a more suitable 'toff' for a boy-friend, and they eventually married.

Dick was (initially), paying me cash at the end of each week. I would immediately trot up to M&S on Camden High Street and buy another shirt, underpants and socks. Despite Julia's, sister's boyfriend doctor's proclamation, my rash had now started to affect my hair—Alopecia Areata was the diagnosis.

Alan Hughes who was fighting a losing battle against a receding hairline, recommended a Trichology Clinic in South Kensington. Once a week, I would slip off there during the office lunch break. There is no cure for Alopecia Areata. All you can do is get as healthy as possible and reduce the stress in your life. The clinic was great and I would come out of there feeling very relaxed. Eventually, the Alopecia disappeared and I no longer looked like a mangy dog.

Angus again came to my rescue transport wise—he gave me an old Hillman Minx car, referred to affectionately as 'Stanley the Steamer.' I soon learned why. The radiator was completely blocked with gunge. Boiling water and caustic soda (more or less), sorted it out. One night, I was out late drinking and driving home in Stanley, I experimented with taking bends, fast. There is a stretch of road behind Finsbury Park with no houses—just walls. As it was late, there was no one around. So I thought, I can only kill myself. Taking a bend too fast I finally got it to skid but, unfortunately, it straightened up and before I could correct, I hit a lamp post—not too fast, and when I got out to inspect the damage, it didn't seem too bad. It was making a terrible noise though, so I thought hell, I've had enough of this naff car anyway . . . so I walked away and left it.

After two or three days of travelling around on the bus and tube, I thought,

"Bugger this for a game of soldiers."
And went back to where I had left the car.

London II

It was still there. I bent the front grill out a bit—the horrible noise stopped, and off I drove again. It was such an uncool car—two-tone powder blue and grey. I was embarrassed to be seen in it by anyone I knew—especially any woman I might have designs on, for example.

Then, Gordon contacted us from Boston, to say he and Cindy were coming to do the UK-European Tour. By this time, Stephanie and I were on the point of breaking up and she was spending most of her time in Bradford. She came to London and we hired a proper (Ford Cortina), car and drove to meet them at Southampton docks—Gordon was terrified of flying, so they crossed the Atlantic on the old liner, SS France.
I was full of anticipation, as I had secretly harboured a strong sexual desire for Cindy, since the time Stephanie and I had stayed temporarily in their flat. Given her strange relationship with Gordon and the fact Steph and I were—more or less—over, I felt there was an opportunity approaching . . . .

We are on the dockside, bunting flying all around us and there is Gordon, waving from the ship. But . . . hold on . . . I can't see Cindy . . .

"Where is Cindy?" I said to Steph.
Then, we see Gordon seems to have some guy with him . . .
It turns out, in the short period since him telling us, he

and Cindy were coming to the UK—Gordon had come out—the guy next to him (Rick) was his partner. I was downhearted but not entirely surprised—Gordon always seemed quite camp. So back we drove to our double bedsit, to be kept awake half the night, by the squeaking sounds of their sexual antics. Fortunately, the room was large and they were in the bed on the other side of the room—even so, we had to demand they stop the noise, so we could sleep.

Eventually, to our relief they set off to Europe on the train from Victoria, and Stephanie returned to Bradford. While Stephanie was still up North, Rick returned alone—they had broken up.

After an awkward couple of days, with me having to entertain him (not in bed, I would like to make perfectly clear), it was a relief when Rick finally returned to Boston. I never did see or hear from Gordon again. For all I know, he could still be pottering around Europe. Peace and equilibrium returned—but not for long.

I had some great times working at N&N. It was a small group of about a dozen people, and it was like being part of a big happy family—though perhaps not all the time. We had some fantastic parties there.

There were some nice ladies working there, and the bosses daughter was attractive too. She had a crush on me, which was a bit awkward—I don't think Dick and

London II

Pam fancied me as their son-in-law. We circled around each other for a while, and (much later), I did date her a couple of times. One of Dick's sons worked in the studio and there was some tension between the two of us—he resented that he was not in a more superior role, above people like me. Especially later, when I was made a junior partner.

Along with Gill Scott, I became a senior member of the design team implementing the new British Airways Corporate Identity. I was responsible for all Three-dimensional aspects of the scheme—interior design, signing, aircraft, vehicle and ground equipment liveries and aircraft interiors.

A typical project for me was the design of a modular, prototype ticket office, shop-fitting system.

There was some discussion by the client, as to where the prototype office would be installed. Brazil, Paris and Rome were mentioned, but of course, they chose (of all places), Bradford, Yorkshire. On the completion day, the Bradford 'Telegraph & Argos' documented my fifteen minutes of fame—the local Pudsey boy made good.

I loved working on the aircraft fleet interiors and exterior livery. Looking back, there was a complete lack of security around the LHR engineering base. I could just drive to the base, park outside one of the technical blocks, and enter without challenge. It always gave me a slight thrill to walk along a corridor, pass through a normal-looking door, and then suddenly, find yourself in this huge, hanger building—the instant change of scale was so dramatic. There could be a 747—in the process of being resprayed in the new livery, surrounded by scaffolding and wrapped in masking tape and brown paper. Strange sight—like an extremely large parcel, waiting to be mailed off somewhere.

With all the interior fittings stripped out, the interior of a 747 was absolutely huge, and never ceased to amaze me.

When I was designing a new, replacement interior for Concorde, I was able to explore her at will and sit in the pilot's seat. The Concorde had originally been delivered with a usual American interior design scheme, featuring multi-coloured fabrics, designed to conceal vomit. I think they were also trying to reassure passengers (with the familiar interior), that it was not unusual or scary to fly on Concorde.

But feed-back told BA passengers were disappointed, that an aircraft looking so fantastic and futuristic on the outside, looked like shit on the inside. My brief was to produce a more appropriate, modern interior. The scheme had to be introduced piecemeal, as the Concorde flight schedule could not be interrupted. In order to make a profit, Concorde, along with the whole conventional aircraft fleet, had to be kept in the air—ideally full of passengers—as long as possible, day and night with 747s and the like. The new scheme emulated the look of smaller executive jets, with leather applied to bulkhead surfaces and with just one colour of fabric for the seats. To offset the relative narrowness of the seats, the fabric was horizontally striped and armrests were upholstered with leather, to match the bulkheads

I flew to America to visit a specialist manufacturer of lightweight materials, for bulkheads and other areas. I had to fly on a 747 (tourist class), to Washington DC and then a local flight to Cleveland. I was disappointed as Concorde was flying to Washington then and I could have done the trip in style and gained a 'meaningful' insight into the Concorde experience!

It was tourist class both ways, with some horrible little kid kicking me in the back the whole time.

The company I was visiting were based in Kent State Ohio and this was shortly after the Campus riots when four students were shot dead and several others wounded. After the contractor had picked me up from the airport, we drove through there, and (to me), the atmosphere felt dark and spooky. The cost of materials for Concorde was breathtaking and proved a limitation on what could be done to improve the interior. Even applying the livery to the exterior was restricted by the fact that—during flight, air friction generated heat, and Concorde expanded twelve inches in length. We produced a lighter version of the BA logotype, and couldn't have the usual blue underbelly—this was a good thing because it looked so much better in its all-white scheme.

I spent my first night in an actual 'Motel.' It was late night when I arrived, but people were swimming in the pool. It was just like in the movies—very American and somewhat thrilling to me then.

Kate

After Stephanie and I had gone our separate ways, Kate and I got together again. I had to contact her as I'd left some of my Doug Binder paintings with her for safekeeping, when I went to America. We started seeing each other again and she became a regular visitor to the studio. As well as her day job, she was working some evenings in the Island Queen Pub in Islington. For a brief period, I had a flat in St Peters Street, close to the pub, so I could go in there and get the occasional free pint. It was a great pub and became my local for a long time, even when I moved out of the area. It was known for its internal décor—larger than life mannequins and huge, hand-painted mirrors. It also served great food.

We both became members of the darts team at the pub next door to the studio. Sometimes, we had away matches at other pubs, which could be fun. One slightly strange night, we competed against the male and female warden's teams at Pentonville Prison, located not far from our office. It was a bit spooky—I think they thought we were all 'Hippies.' The previous time I'd been in that prison, was to visit Kate's brother, Steve—a troubled soul.

We had good and bad times together—some turbulent times . . . Kate was beautiful, exciting, had style and was bright, but she had a short fuse, and was—to say the least—a trifle highly strung. We were living in a flat above a butchers shop, in Brecknock Road N7, walking distance from my workplace. The staff in the butcher's shop were great, they would buzz our doorbell whenever traffic wardens were approaching our car, and I would rush down to move it. There was an off-licence just across the road and I would pop in there on a Friday night, to buy a bottle of my favourite tipple Valpolicella, for £1—an average price for a bottle of wine in those days. Somehow we acquired a cat who we called May.

This was a grotty area of London and on weekends, we would be watching TV or listening to music, to the accompaniment of beer bottles being thrown up and down Brecknock Road. Stephanie phoned me at the studio one day and told me she was going to work in New York, and would like to meet up before she left. Given I was now seeing Kate (who would quite likely take exception to such a meeting) and not wanting any complications, I declined and felt ashamed of my cowardice. It turned out us breaking up was the best thing that ever happened to Stephanie—while she was in New York, she met and married a multimillionaire art dealer. When he died, she inherited a great deal of money. She is now living somewhere in England, with her new American partner.

I was now the proud owner of a (second-hand), White Ford Cortina estate car, courtesy of my bank manager—Mr Barron. He was such a nice man. This was in the days when you actually had a living-breathing person, as your manager. He supported Peter, Michael and me through the BFB Design days and now said to me, without any prompting,

"You must have a need for a car, take £500 and
buy yourself something nice."

It was a good car and made several trips up North before I suggested to Kate, we have a holiday in France. We set off to down France to visit my old haunt, Ramatuelle. We couldn't afford to rent the house I'd worked on, so we agreed to sleep in the car. I arranged a foam mattress in the back, and along with the stereo cassette system, the car was a regular home-from-home. We thus avoided hotel bills.

It took a couple of days or so to get there using the ordinary 'D' roads, but the sleeping arrangement worked well. We would stop in some town for dinner and then drive to the outskirts of town until we found a quiet spot to pull over and bed down for the night. After arriving in Ramatuelle, all went well for a while, but then Kate started kicking up a fuss—about what, I cannot recall. I doubt if I knew then.

We would drive up into hills above the village where we had found a place to park in the trees, away from the track. Hidden from view, we could look down on the village below, and Pampelonne Beach beyond.

One evening, there was such torrential rain—Kate stripped off naked, got out of the car, and had a shower in the rain. After a moment's hesitation, I joined her. Best shower I have ever had. It went from bad to worse between us, to the extent that I told her I was going to drive to Nice and put her on a flight back to London. This seemed to resolve the situation for the better, and we continued with the rest of the holiday together.

Another evening, we had dinner in a smart restaurant on the port in St Tropez. When we had finished eating, Kate got out her paraphernalia and started rolling up a cigarette. This attracted a great deal of interest from other diners, and I felt embarrassed. I was still unsure of myself in such situations—lacking confidence.

Kate was always fearless—she didn't give a damn what anyone might think of her. At least, that's the impression she gave. It may have been false bravado. Prior to our relationship, she had been involved with an affluent man, who had paid for her to stay in the very best London hotels. In contrast, at that time I had never stayed in a swanky hotel and would have felt out of my depth doing so.

Back in Brecknock, the relationship continued to be volatile. One evening we were out to dinner at a restaurant in Primrose Hill, when I said something (I cannot recall what), she took an exception to, and ran out of the restaurant in a rage. I followed and a stand-up-knock-down fight ensued in the street—nothing to cause injury to either of us, just a lot of slapping and verbal insults being exchanged.

Then a Good Samaritan intervened and, after I told him (politely) to mind his own business, he (or someone else), called the police. They arrived quick time in a squad car. However, once they had reassured themselves we were not about to kill each other, they left us to wander off home. The police had been told a male was assaulting some poor, defenceless woman—it was more likely, the other way round.

Then, a little later, Kate came to the studio for lunch. We were sitting in the pub (next door to the office) when she said to me,

"I think we should get married."

I was somewhat taken aback—confused and speechless. I hated the idea of seeming weak, being afraid of a challenge, afraid of saying no. I always acted spontaneously whenever a challenge or exciting opportunity presented itself—so yes, I was afraid to say no, afraid of what her reaction might be.

So I said,

"Okay then. Let's do it."

When I told him we were to marry, Angus was bemused. He said,

"Just last week, you were saying how crazy she is and you were going to finish it for good?"

I know, I know. It is a fact—I seem to find strong women attractive. Meek and mild women (no matter how attractive) quickly lose their allure and I end up treating them badly. Does every male-female relationship have to be like this? Can two mutually strong—or weak—partners have a successful relationship?

The wedding was quickly arranged, before either of us had a chance to change our mind. We lied about our home address (giving a friend's) so we could marry at Hampstead Registry Office—rather than Kings Cross—not at all salubrious, especially with all the working girls hanging around the streets. The night before the wedding, we (of course) had a terrible row and ended up sleeping on the floor for the few remaining hours of the night.

There was a good crowd of family and friends and after the ceremony, we all went up to the Spaniards for drinks. With twenty close friends and family, we then went on for lunch at Fredericks in Camden Passage.

Kate

In the evening we had a party at Brecknock that was a great success—apart from Angus offending my boss Dick Negus. Angus was relating the story of our Brighton Queens hotel project, and how the hotel was full of creeps having dirty weekends with ladies of questionable repute—Dick himself was fond of spending the odd weekend at the Queens to chill-out, but he didn't let on to Angus—I wanted the ground to open up beneath me.

The next day, we drove to Brighton for a brief honeymoon, staying at the Grand Hotel—my first swanky hotel and yes, I did feel uncomfortable—out of my depth. At dinner in the hotel dining room, the wine waiter brought our drinks on a silver tray. I didn't realise that I was supposed to tip him separately to the actual meal. He returned to his colleague and muttered (loudly enough that I could hear),

"Look at this, nothing!"

What an arsehole he was. Thank God all that tipping bullshit has gone. France led the way with the adding of service charge before it was adopted in the UK.

We had walks along the seafront and on the Pier, arcade people calling out,

"Come on, have a go at shooting the mother in law."

Was it that obvious?

Kate was a jealous woman and being out and about with her, could (at times) be quite an ordeal. If she for one moment suspected I had glanced at another woman in the street, she would go into orbit. It's difficult to be in a social situation or simply just walking around town, and avoid catching a glimpse of a women—I tried walking while looking up at the sky. This was not a practical solution.

We started looking for a house to buy and eventually ended up in Victoria Road, Alexander Palace. The house had seven rooms, all set up as individual bedsits. And so I set about converting it back to a family house—it took eleven years, which was exactly the duration of our marriage.

Every spare minute and every spare penny I had was spent on the house. One day at the office, Kate turned up after having lunch with a friend—she was a bit tipsy. It seemed she was pregnant and the whole office knew about it before me—I was told in front of several work colleagues. I felt very unhappy about this, not the pregnancy, but the fact she had told me in such a manner. It could have been, should have been, a private and intimate moment. The pregnancy was not planned. I don't recall us ever discussing children. Maybe this is why she made the public announcement—perhaps she thought I would want her to have an abortion. It would not have been so.

So, nine months later in early summer, Lucy Anne was born. Kate seemed happy during the first year with Lucy, sitting out in the garden on sunny days,

Kate

while I worked in the garden. I loved reworking the garden—at times it was too much of a distraction from the necessary work on the house.

In the winter of that first year, Kate turned up at the studio with Lucy in her arms. She had been visiting a friend and wanted to get a lift home with me. We left the studio at 6:00pm, just as it was starting to snow. The journey would normally take fifteen to twenty minutes—it took six hours, getting home at midnight. It snowed so heavily that within minutes, the roads were gridlocked. Lucy breastfed and slept, the whole time. Nothing we could do, but stick it out.

We went to Devon and Cornwall for a couple of holidays. On one occasion, driving down in the Cortina, the engine decided it had done enough and completely gave up. With the help of the AA, we finally arrived late at night, with the car behind us, on a trailer. Next day, I took it to a local garage to learn that it needed a new 'Short Engine'. Then I had to go to the local branch of my bank, to see if I could borrow the money to pay for the work. Fortunately, the bank agreed and I was able to get the work done. Unfortunately, this meant that we spent the holiday confined to one spot—only receiving the car back, the day before we were due to return to London. Driving back, the gearbox then decided to play up, and it had to be held in gear all the time.

Back in London, I bought a reconditioned gearbox and

fitted it in the street, outside our house—I like to think Des was looking over my shoulder.

I had no preference for the child's sex when Lucy was born. Later, Kate used to look after a neighbours young boy and he would often watch me working on various DIY tasks around the house, asking questions. I found myself thinking how nice it would be to have my own son watching me. So, plans for Daniel were put into action. Books were read and old wives tales listened to. A selection of methods was followed, all (of course) involving sex.

It may be a coincidence, but eventually a boy—Daniel was born. We had chosen not to know the babies sex but if it was a boy, he was going to be called Daniel James. As soon as he popped out, and the midwife held him aloft, I was overwhelmed with happiness and blurted out,

"It's a boy, it's a boy . . ."

Kate said,

"Oh, alright then, we'll call him Norman."

(after my father). I was moved and grateful to her. The saying—old men and babies look alike is true. So it was Daniel James Norman.

Kate's volatility continued to be a problem. We went on summer vacation to Ramatuelle with Kate's sister Megs, and friends and neighbours Howard and Sue, who also had a young child. It was a nightmare, with disagreements and arguments, resulting in the end of the friendship. The next year we again went to Ramatuelle, this time with friends John and Wendy. Again, it was a nightmare and the end of the friendship.

Negus & Negus were commissioned by Pakistan International Airways, to design their new corporate identity. I produced a design scheme for their ticket office interiors. Working on their flagship Ticket Shop in Karachi, involved me flying out there once a month.

On my first trip there, while walking around in the streets, I was disconcerted to see what I thought was blood splattered around on the pavements, and there were armed guards outside all the important buildings—worrying. Later I learned it wasn't blood; it was Betel Nuts chewed by the locals and then the juice, spat out.

Visiting the local contractors who were making the interior fittings, was an interesting experience—like taking a trip back in time. I was watching one of the carpenters drilling holes, in ticket sales desk—to my amazement, he was using an ancient 'Bow' drill, moving it back and forward. The materials we take for granted in the west like Formica for instance, were unavailable and had to be imported from Russia.

Despite all my precautions, on the third trip, I got a stomach bug. Of course, the hotel toilet chose this moment to stop working. It was all quite nasty. The PIA medical officer came to visit me and gave me a tablet, which blocked me up, so to speak, and allowed me to eventually fly back home.

Back in London, I woke up one morning in acute pain. Our GP came to see me and immediately had me whisked into isolation hospital. It was typhoid, and I was there for a few days. This was during the Bhutto era, and when he was hanged in 1979, my last two scheduled trips were cancelled. I was relieved, but (at the same time), disappointed that I didn't get to see the finished project.

For a long time, an office colleague Gilly was trying to get me to try playing squash with her, but I kept putting her off. Then, one day I agreed to give it a try. A group of us met at the club and, although I only got about ten minutes on the court, I instantly became a convert. From that day on, it was squash, squash and more squash.

At the height of this new love affair, I was playing daily—sometimes twice daily. I had put on a lot of weight during the early days of the marriage, and squash—along with running at weekends and cycling to work every day, got me back in shape. I was training to enter the first ever London Marathon, but when it came to application time, it was so oversubscribed, I didn't get a place.

January 1981, my sister Sylvia phoned me at the office, to tell me Dad was in Leeds Infirmary.

"It's nothing serious, no need for you to worry, but I thought you should know anyway."

Kate

I spent that Friday evening, debating whether to go up to see him. Saturday morning I was on the train to Leeds, arriving there at lunchtime. Dad seemed pretty out of it. I told him to carry on sleeping, while I sat, holding his hand.

Later in the afternoon, Mum, Marie, Des and Eddie arrived to visit, and were surprised to find me there. Later, Dad managed to sit in a chair while the nurse changed the bedding—he didn't seem too bad then. Eventually, we all had to leave.

Des had taken up tennis and I had played with him before, on previous visits—quite embarrassing I remember, as me being a regular squash player, I decided I would be able to show him and his friends a thing or two. Every time I hit the ball—it went either into the net or completely out of the court. Not the same as squash at all. We arranged to play next morning, when I hoped I would do better.

Sunday morning at nine o'clock, he comes into my bedroom, waking me to say,

"Your Dad's died, during the night."

The funeral was on Tuesday, and after spending a couple of days with Marie and Sylvia, I returned to London. Marie was close to Dad and she took his death badly. I myself drew some comfort from having made the trip to see him, and being able to spend those few hours, holding his hand.

Dick Negus and I were asked by PIA to go to Lisbon,

Past Tense

Portugal, to inspect the interiors of two 747s they were buying from TAP-the Portuguese national airline. We got an early morning BA flight, but unfortunately, because Lisbon airport was closed by fog, we were diverted to Porto.

We were just dumped there and the flight returned to London. Porto had suffered terrorist bombings a few days earlier, so I wasn't too happy finding myself there. Fortunately, a local BA agent was travelling with us and he organised a bus to take us to Lisbon. This was an ordinary, everyday type of bus and was consequently, not at all comfortable. The journey took hours. This was the time of the Portuguese exodus from Angola, and when we arrived in Lisbon late that night, the hotel was full of refugees. I had some food and went to bed exhausted, and with a splitting headache.

After breakfast the next day we set off to the airport to inspect the aircraft. To my dismay, I realised my passport was still at the hotel reception desk. I was then raced back to the hotel in the TAP car that had been placed at our disposal—I say raced, but the fog was still thick.

Finally, I arrived back at the airport and was able to board the two 747s sitting in the hanger building, shrouded in fog— spooky. I now had just an hour left to inspect the two aircraft interiors, before we had to get the return flight to London.

There was a lot of doubt as to whether the flight would

leave, given the heavy fog. I was particularly anxious, as the aircraft was due to take off down the same runway I had (just a short while ago) been zooming around on in the fog, with the TAP driver.

Dick and I were sat on the two front seats, close to the cockpit door. The cockpit door was open all the time during taxiing, take off and throughout the whole flight. Looking through the door straight out of the cockpit windows, and seeing nothing but fog as we hurtled down the runway, was quite alarming. Security wise, it is all different now.

In order to avoid the complete replacement of their BAC 1-11 aircraft fleet and to compete with the wide-body aircraft that had started operating on some of their routes, British Caledonian chose to have them re-designed to have the 'wide-bodied' look of their competitors. This allowed them to extend the operating period for a number of years.

We got this project under false pretences. I had done some aircraft interior design sketches for PIA, so they assumed I was an 'Aircraft Interior Designer'. When BCAL (who were assisting PIA with their computer systems) asked if they knew of such a person, PIA suggested N&N. The first couple of meetings with the BCAL Engineers at Gatwick engineering base were quite tricky, but we were able to convince them we really did know what we were doing. The trick I had already learned was to keep quiet and listen, learn the jargon, and then feed it back to them like a long time expert. Never the less, we went on to do a good job for them.

We then designed a new corporate identity for City & Guilds, and I designed a series of travelling exhibitions for the Centenary Year. When all the preparations were complete, myself and other members of the project team were lined up, for presentation to the Guilds Patron—HR Highness the Duke of Edinburgh. I was impressed by the precision of the proceedings—everything happened exactly when it should. He arrived at exactly the predicted time; he took exactly the allotted time for shaking everyone's hand and he left at exactly the predicted time.

The next day there was a special service at St Paul's Cathedral, and Prince Phillip read the sermon. All very impressive at the time—to me anyway.

Later, we were commissioned to design the branding for the labour breakaway SDP Party, and I designed the stage set for the press launch. It was an exciting day, and I was eventually sad when the Political venture failed.

One evening, Kate decided she would like to learn chess, so I agreed to give her some tuition. We sat down and I set up the board, showing her the basic moves. So then, we start a game . . . After ten minutes or so, I make the fatal mistake of smirking (or appearing to smirk) at some move she made—suddenly, it was raining chess pieces. This was the end of Kate's bid to be a chess 'Grand Master.'

She was fiercely independent, proud and could not bear to seem weak or dependent on any man—certainly not me. She once told me,

"She thought I was arrogant, and needed taking down a peg or two."

Well, she certainly did just that.

My attempt to teach her to drive had a similar result, although it lasted a bit longer—about twenty minutes. We were just sat in the car, outside the house. When I said (I do not recall what), she exploded and jumped out of the car. I was just going through the basics—check the handbrake, check the gears are in neutral etc. We agreed she should get lessons from a driving school. She did and eventually, passed the test.

She then tried her best to wreck my beloved Cortina. After being out by herself one evening, she had an accident. The next day, I had to go and recover the car—it was un-drivable and had to be brought home on a trailer. Outside the house, in the street again—this time to replace the front anti-roll bar and a damaged wheel. I guessed she had hit a traffic bollard. My employers then decided to give me one of their cars—an Alpha Sud. Very nice. Kate then did a repeat performance with the Alpha, but this time she managed to drive it home. Two destroyed tyres and damaged wheel rims. I don't remember what explanation I gave, but my employers paid for the repairs and new tyres.

Kate never seemed quite the same after Daniels birth—possibly a touch of 'Post Natal Depression.' It was never discussed, and our relationship continued to degenerate.

After one particular argument, she through a pepper grinder at me—it hit low down, and hurt—and said,

"I need some space."

Yeah, that old line. She arranged for me to swap places with her sister Megs, who lived a couple of miles away. I could visit the children on weekends, while Kate was absent.

One Saturday morning, as I was leaving to visit the children, Kate's mum (who lived next door to Megs) was on her way to Wood Green, so I gave her a lift. In the slow high street traffic, I saw Kate queuing at a cash machine with a bloke.

"Oh look," I said.

"There's Kate with her boyfriend."

Kate's mum said,

"I'm not saying anything, Stewart."

She obviously knew. I dropped her off, and she must have told Kate she was rumbled. She came straight home and admitted she was having an affair.

She said,

"It isn't over, this doesn't mean the end, we can share."

Kate

Desperate to keep the marriage going, I agreed. But when it came to it, she would not share. She refused to give him up and left me no option, but to instigate separation.

Although I was now a junior partner at N&N, after eleven years I was unhappy with the type of work we were doing—there wasn't enough 3-dimensional work coming my way, so I resigned. This coincided exactly with the end of my marriage. March 1984. I guess the two events were linked and I felt I just couldn't go on in the same way. Everything had to change. So no job, no wife—I think this is called starting with a clean slate. Given that I was also starting my new life as an independent designer, with an uncertain future income, there was no way I could finance two different homes as well as a new business.

We agreed to split everything 50/50, house, furniture, books and records, everything. It's strange how after eleven years of hard work on the house, getting it just the way we wanted it, it no longer seemed important. I suppose if I'm honest, I couldn't bear the thought of her lover moving into the house and my shoes—so to speak.

My share from the house got me through the first year of my new design practice.

I managed to find a room in the flat of a work colleague's friend. Kate went to stay with her sister until she found her own place through a council, housing association. On the final day of leaving the house, I had left the double-bed base and legs leaning against a wall, ready for loading into the van.

Kate arrived with Daniel, and before I could stop him, he ran into the room and managed to pull the base down on top of himself. Fortunately, the legs were long enough to prevent the main base from landing on him, but one of the legs caught his hand.

Off we rushed with him to the A&E. He was okay, with no broken bones. It was a strange conclusion to our final hours of marriage.

The room I was renting was barely big enough for my bed and my stereo. Everything else went into storage. Leo—an American Greek was my landlord. He was a nice guy, but he had a slightly crazy girlfriend and they were always fighting. A couple of times they brought the fight into my room—One night I was lying in bed, listening to music and the first one would burst in, look and leave, and then the other would, saying,

"If you're going to look, then I am!"

Strange times.

After a year and a couple of failed attempts to buy my own place, I bought a top floor flat in Stoke Newington. There was a hole in the roof, a huge wasp's nest in the loft, and it needed a lot of other work too.

Kate would drop Lucy and Daniel off every Friday evening and I would take them back Sunday. We had some fun times together those weekends. The routine was we would first visit the local video shop and choose three VHS tapes for the weekend viewing. They would come to the squash club with me and play with other children there. My good friend Eric's daughter Jude would often be there, and they would play together. One of my fondest memories is of (on Sundays, before taking them back) bathing them both together, and then brushing their hair in front of the TV—Lucy's was long, but I got good at removing the tangles.

Sometimes, when Kate dropped the kids off, she would stay and have drinks with me in the kitchen, while they were in the living room watching TV. Eventually, one of the kids would come into the kitchen and instruct Kate to leave as they only had the weekend to spend with Dad, and she was using up their time. Sometimes those kitchen drinks would get a bit out of hand.

Lucy's school organised a day trip to Calais and rising early, I drove Lucy to catch the Coach outside the school. The children were boarding the coach, but when it came to Lucy, they asked for her passport— she did not have it. The teacher said,

"I am sorry, but you can't go without your pass port."

The look on Lucy's face was heart breaking. It hurts to see such intense disappointment on your child's face. I decided we could go get her passport from Kate and then drive to Dover, to meet the coach there. We overtook the coach about halfway there. It was not my intention to go with Lucy, but she persuaded me to go along on the trip. It was a pleasant day out and Lucy and I had fun together, despite me having a bad headache. I often got headaches in those days—I wonder why. I have some nice photos of her playing on the beach there.

It was around this time I decided to get an image makeover, in the form of some subtle highlights in my hair. In the Wood Green Unisex Salon, I had what appeared to be a giant condom put on my head. It had lots of tiny holes in it, through which they pulled tufts of hair. The result I was trying to achieve was as if I had been in the sun and my hair had become slightly bleached—sitting there in front of the large mirror, I felt and looked stupid. An embarrassing and a never to be repeated experience.

The squash club became a saviour for me. It was a friendly club, with lots of nice people—we had regular social events and this helped me a great deal. I also had encounters with two or three women there.

Today I still have friends I met there. One woman, I really liked was Glenda. We got on well and the sex was good. The relationship lasted for a while, but the trouble was she had this terrible habit of criticising the food in every restaurant I took her. On our first meal together, one night after the squash club, I took her to the local Greek I was fond of eating in. She was critical of the food. I thought the food was fine and I considered it rude of her, to express such an opinion. If someone bought me a meal, no matter how dismal the food might be, I would not be so rude. Finally, one weekend, she drove down from Norfolk, where she was now working and we went for a meal. Same again . . . I flipped, saying she had ruined the evening and off she drove back to Norfolk, never to be seen again.

The first summer after the separation, Lucy and I went to Ramatuelle together—Kate considered Daniel was too young to make the journey. We drove down in my new Suzuki jeep—not so fast, meaning a couple of overnight stays were required on the journey. We did the first part of the journey on the old roads, but then switched to the auto-route, to save time. I had bought two new tape cassettes—Elvis Costello – 'King of America' and Paul Simon – 'Graceland'. We played them none stop, all the way down through France.

We had some nice times together, although I occasionally felt a bit down due to the marriage failure, so perhaps wasn't as much fun for Lucy as I should have been. Before leaving, we went to the local winemaking, cooperative and bought four Demijohns of the local Ramatuelle wine I loved so much. It was great buying wine there—it was like going to a petrol station, with pumps dispensing wine instead of petrol. So cheap. Driving back we had to cross over the Massif des

Past Tense

Maures, mountains. Suddenly, we could smell wine—two of the demijohns had burst, the bottoms completely separated. This had happened before on the previous trips, but I still didn't understand why.

It was later when the obvious explanation occurred to me—the Massif des Maures were over eight hundred metres high, with a correspondingly lower atmospheric pressure. The wine was bottled at sea level . . . Duh . . . Too late now.

SRBA

After the separation from Kate and N&N, I rented desk space in an Architect's office in Camden Town. They were nice people and I had pleasant times there, both socially and work-wise. My desk space was a table and drawing board located face to face with an identical desk, occupied by JT, the senior architect of the company. We could reach out and touch each other. It could have been claustrophobic, but he was a nice guy and he seemed to like me, so we got on well.

As Christmas and the usual parties approached, there was talk (I can't put my finger on it) about his wife and how she would like me. I really can't remember or understand why this was. The architects on the floor below ours held a party to which I turned up late, after briefly attending another office party. The minute I walked into the room JT's wife approached me and we began dancing. After about ten minutes she was

206

kissing me passionately—I hasten to add, JT was not there. She was attractive and I was somewhat taken aback. We ended up in the roof garden, where heavy petting took place. After the party, I gave her a lift home and she insisted I come in. I was sitting on the sofa and she was reclining across me. Knowing her husband was upstairs (hopefully asleep) made me feel uneasy, to say the least. After a while I was able to leave, without any drama occurring.

During the following days at the office, I felt very uneasy sitting close, face to face with JT. We subsequently had two or three social occasions involving the office. JT always seemed perfectly relaxed, suggesting that his wife should sit next to me. I began to wonder if perhaps he liked watching—it never came to that. Sometime later, JT left the company. His replacement was a strange fellow, whom I did not really take to.

There was a female architect working there, whom I was keen on, and I think she liked me. Trouble was, the replacement was obviously crazy about her too, and he was constantly hindering my attempts to get up close and personal with her. One evening we were working late and he eventually left, leaving just the two of us—I thought this is my chance. But bugger me, if he didn't come back and persuade her to accept a lift home. He must have been sat in his car, worrying about what might transpire in the office. We never did get together.

I was there for a year until (due to lack of work) the Architect could no longer afford the lease, and decided to continue working from home. Two Architects, Peter and Steven, were also renting desks there, so along with Derek, a Quantity Surveyor we knew, the four of us decided to set up our own communal workspace. We found a light industrial loft in Shoreditch and completely refitted it. The finished result was impressive and we called it—'Shoreditch Studio.'
It was on an eleven-year lease, which (later) became a problem as the recession arrived, and things got very tough for the architectural and design industry.

Now, Fortune smiled on me for the third time—while all around me were suffering, I received a phone call from British Airways. They wanted me to survey and redesign, every 'Ticket Shop' they had in the whole British Isles—one hundred and fifty. One of my studio colleagues was Scottish. He surveyed the Scotland locations, another was Irish and so he did Belfast and Dublin. I hired a fast BMW and drove like a 'Bat out of Hell' all over England and Wales, and flew to the Channel Islands. As this was before I had a CAD system, I hired ten year-out architectural students to crash out drawings. The drawings and specification package was ready to go out to tender, when BA pulled the plug on the whole project. I was paid, so what the heck. I think they realised that the days of Ticket Shops were numbered and in future, everything would be done by call centres and eventually online.

I have since done the same amount of work with just one or two assistants. It's amazing how much technology assisted, small design practices like mine. Looking back, it's hard to believe how long we took to decide whether we needed a FAX machine, or not. There was no email and all our correspondence had to be typed by the studio secretary, on an IBM golf-ball typewriter.

After Kate, I was looking for sexual reassurance and I managed to put myself about a bit, having pleasant encounters with some nice women. Rosie phoned me one evening from Bradford. She too had been dumped by her husband. She had heard I was in the same position and suggested we meet up when she came to London. We met up and spent the weekend together. She came to London a couple of times a month, and I also visited her in the north one time. She was such a nice woman and deserved to be happy. Unfortunately, it turned out I was not to be the one who would make her happy.

On 22 August 1985, British Airways 737 had an engine fire during the take-off roll. Fifty-Three passengers perished along with two members of the cabin crew. Most of the deaths were due to smoke inhalation. The next day, I get a call to a meeting at British Airways. They asked me to design the interior of the EPIC (Emergency Procedure Information Centre) located in the basement of an LHR technical block. The centre is manned by BA volunteers and—to speak plainly, its purpose is to deal with anxious relatives, identify the living, identify the dead and try to identify . . . body parts. The basement was a terrible gloomy environment, desperately needing refurbishment. I did a great scheme I was proud of, but when the costs came in, they shelved it. I was told this happened every time they *'dropped one'*, as they say in the airline industry, but when the fuss has died down, refurbishment schemes are quietly forgotten.

When British Airways acquired British Caledonian Airline, I spent a year visiting the whole West Coast of Africa, converting all the BCAL facilities to BA corporate standards. I would spend a week in London working while I acquired two visas and then a BA flight to the first Country. After two or three days, surveying, designing and commissioning local project Architects, I would then get a local flight to the next country. Then a BA flight back to London.

Everywhere I went throughout Africa, I had to evaluate the manufacturing capabilities of the local contractors. Everyone I visited had the same sales pitch,

"We can make anything and everything you want."

What I quickly came to realise was—they meant as long it was Japanese type lacquer finish. Formica was not an option. Consequently, it was decided to import all furniture and fittings. That of course, created more problems—customs delays. This was exacerbated by BA management's instructions that no bribes were to be paid. Much to the frustration of the local BA personnel. Bribery was the norm—it was just how things worked. Several of the countries I visited, disintegrated into Bloody civil war not long after. I began to wonder if I was a jinx.

Then Alan Sugar came on the scene, and I acquired an Amstrad 1512 PC. Later, this was replaced by a proper CAD system and I was able to produce more work, more quickly and to a higher professional standard.

It was around this time I met my second wife to be—Yasmine. She was a friend of Leo, the person I had been renting the room from. He phoned me one day to ask if I would give some advice to a friend of his, who was 'artistic.' She did not turn up for the first meeting, we had arranged. However eventually, we did meet up at the studio. This beautiful Eurasian girl—half Bangladeshi, half German—arrived. I was very taken with her. Her drawings and paintings were good and displayed a natural creative talent. She was eighteen years younger than me and (I believed) clearly out of my league. Consequently, I never had any thoughts of making advances.

While there was nothing I could offer her employment-wise, I suggested if she wanted to learn more about design, she could attend one of the seminars at the Chartered Society of Designers—of which I was a fellow. She had missed the first, but there were another two remaining.

"Yes", she said.

I didn't expect her to turn up but to my surprise, she did. She also came to the final one, after which we had a meal together. Again, while enjoying her company and admiring her beauty, I did not have any expectations. Then, saying good night, she gave me a gift. It was a nicely designed automatic drafting pencil, in an attractive case. There was a card containing the following words,

"Thank you for your help, kindness, consideration and understanding. And who knows what else. "

Those last five words . . . without which, my life from that point on would have been quite different. Possibly in some ways good, but definitely bad, in that I would not have my two beautiful daughters—Manon and Cosima. We started dating—meals, concerts and exhibitions. One day in spring, looking out of the studio kitchen window (it was such a lovely day), I phoned Yasmine and said, 'Why don't we drive to Brighton for lunch?'

"Yes," she said.

Off we went and on arrival in Brighton, I pulled into an underground car park. Just before we got out of the car, she leaned across and kissed me passionately. We had not kissed before—other than on the cheek. Wow (I thought), that's a turn up for the books. We had a lovely day, walking on the beach and pier. In the evening after a meal, we drove back to London and I dropped her off home in Kingston Vale. It was the start of the relationship proper.

Rosie was due in London for an upcoming bank holiday weekend and I knew I had to phone her and tell her I could not see her anymore. She was upset and I felt ashamed.

Yasmine and I went to see the film 'Jean De Floret' and the sequel, 'Manon Des Source.' I found these films moving and was emotional watching them. We began talking about a 'Love Child' and we agreed she would be called Manon. It was all intense and emotional.

On my African trips, I was always desperate to get on the flight back to London—and Yasmine. After a week of hard work in extreme heat and dust, it was wonderful to walk into the 747 first class cabin and be handed a glass of chilled Champagne by a smiling stewardess. All the flights were in and out of Gatwick and Yasmine would always be there to wave me goodbye and to welcome me on my return. My tickets were always business-class out of Gatwick, with the option of an upgrade to first class, but I was never upgraded. On the return flights, I was always given first-class by the local manager, whom I had spent time with during the visit. I hated going to Nigeria, it was just so corrupt. Unfortunately I had to make several visits there. Staying at the Lagos Sheraton was civilised, but other locations, such as Kano—not so. The rooms were shabby and prostitutes knocked on your door, during the night. While staying at the Sheraton and other similar hotels, I developed the routine of having my evening meal delivered to my room and spending the evening (and sometimes much of the night), working on the design layouts for that location. I could then sometimes get to spend the day by the swimming pool, acquiring a suntan, and swimming lengths.

The local internal flights were always a bit scary. One flight I had to take from Port Harcourt to Lagos, was particularly so. Boarding the flight from the apron, passengers were fighting to get up the boarding steps. At the top of the steps, the flight and cabin crew were trying to repel them. My escort while in Nigeria was some kind of tribal Prince and people tended to get out of his way, with me following closely behind.

He was a striking man, handsome and wore Pier Cardin suits with lots of gold jewellery and the obligatory gold Rolex. It was quite funny sometimes, to see how crowds of people parted as he approached, particularly women. 'Moses and the parting of the waves' . . . It certainly made my life easier there.

On this occasion, it worked again and somehow, we

managed to get up the boarding steps. The chaos below continued, the boarding steps were withdrawn and the aircraft departed, almost empty, leaving most of the passengers on the apron. Some of the crew were visibly shaken, which made me feel a trifle nervous. Much to my relief, we landed safely in Lagos. This kind of event was far from unusual—I witnessed more than one furious punch-up at the First Class check-in desks. Also, I was arrested a couple of times while on my own, and had to be rescued by my escort.

These local African flights always filled me with apprehension. I was told the story of Air Nigeria receiving their first 'wide-body' aircraft—they were doing trial 'circuits and bumps' where the aircraft lands and immediately takes off again, this being repeated multiple times. Trouble is, the supervisor omitted to tell the pilot to take off again—so he just went off the end of the runway.

Everywhere you went, there was always some 'official' trying to shake you down, right up to departures at the airport—a security officer would take you in a little booth, draw a curtain and ask you what you had for him. You were not allowed to take any of the currency out of the country—why the hell anybody would want to do so? 'Naira' was worthless paper. The shaky currencies of the various countries I visited, was the main reason BCAL had gone bust and been taken over by BA. They had mountains of local paper money, but they could not get it out of the country, and it was worthless anyway.

I remember in Monrovia, Liberia—they didn't have paper money at all—just coins. Going out for a meal, you had to take long paper tubes of Liberian dollars. When waiting at the airport for my return flight to London, I saw the local BA manager (whom I'd been staying with) walking across the apron with a large briefcase, to give to the flight crew. I knew it was filled with US dollars. BA was selling tickets for US dollars which was illegal, and this was the only way they could get money out of the country.

Liberia was one of those countries that experienced bloody civil war shortly after I left. When I was being driven around between meetings, there would be frequent army checkpoints to negotiate. After dark could be particularly difficult, as off duty-armed soldiers sometimes set up unofficial checkpoints, to extract money from drivers.

Freetown Sierra Leone was an interesting visit. I was met at Lungi International Airport, by the BA Manager and then driven fourteen miles to catch a ferry, across Tagrin Bay, to Freetown. On the journey, he related the story of the million-pound car he was now driving. Because of the crazy currency restrictions and general difficulties importing goods, the (in real terms) cost of importing the car in local currency and allowing for all the bribes etc., was one million pounds.

Past Tense

It didn't matter because it was local currency and basically worthless. Apparently, he had fallen asleep at the wheel and run the previous car off the road late one night, making this same journey.

I had my first and only helicopter flight, from the hotel grounds, direct to the airport. It was an old, rickety Russian machine. Not reliable—I was told (thankfully) afterwards. Sometime later, this country too descended into bloody violence.

In contrast, Abidjan, Cote d'Ivoire, was developed and sophisticated. I went shopping on my first day there, for a tape measure (I had forgotten mine)—in Habitat. Despite the sophistication, there was some unrest after my visit—it must have been me. . .

Much of the West African Coast was unsuitable for tourism, because of the Atlantic swell falling onto the beaches. It was unsafe to swim off most of them.

The couple of beaches I did explore (in the rare, spare moments) were always covered in great globules of oily tar—it was almost impossible not to step in one. I saw several deserted and ruined beach resorts. Also, apart from a few mangy looking monkeys, there is no wild game there. Still, it was a lucrative and interesting experience, but a relief when the project was finally finished. Now I could spend more time with Yasmine. She was so beautiful, intelligent and creative—and . . . good in bed. I thought I'd died and gone to heaven.

My Mother was now living with my Brother Eddie and

his wife Brenda. Eddie thought she would be safer with him. This meant I had to get permission from him to visit mum and stay with them for the weekend—I was used to just turning up whenever the mood took me, knowing my old bedroom was always there waiting for me. After a while, the arrangement ceased to work and mum went into sheltered housing in Pudsey and later, a care home just up the road, from Eddie's house.

I took Yasmine up to meet Mum and family. Mum said,

"Eee, Stewart lad, she's lovely. Make sure you marry her."

We then visited my sister Sylvia in Ripon and early in the conversation, Sylvia said to Yasmine,

"So how long have been with Stewart?"

Yasmine said,

"Oh, four months or so, but I love him very much."

This was not a typical Northern response and I could see Sylvia was a bit taken aback.

"Oh." She said.

It was not much later when (after a fall in the care home) Mum died. She was eighty-five, frail and beginning to show signs of dementia. I drove up alone, to attend the funeral. She was buried in the same grave as Dad and Audrey in Pudsey cemetery. I stayed with Marie for a few days, and Sylvia and her husband

Past Tense

Melvyn spent a little time with us. We had fish 'n chips from the local shop—memories of happier times.

With all the business travelling I was doing, I decided it was time to get one of these new-fangled, mobile phones. Off I went to the Finsbury square Vodafone shop in the city. I bought the latest, nicely designed Nokia phone. It was sitting on the box, while the saleswoman was doing the final paperwork. Two guys enter the shop and start looking at various phones while chatting away. One of them then picks up my phone and, looking straight at me as if challenging me to say something, slips it into his pocket.
I did not challenge him and they left. The saleswoman returns and starts closing the box. I said,

"Is the phone in the box?"
She opens the box and looks around.

"Where is it?" she says.
I tell her about the guys, saying,

"You are welcome to search me if you like. But I don't have it."

Much to my frustration, I had to wait another two weeks for a replacement—and visit the local police station to give evidence. There was no way I was going to be stabbed defending a phone.
During the many, many flights I took on British Airways business, I only ever experienced a couple of inflight incidents. Returning from Hamburg once, with my client, the aircraft started flying very slowly. My

client (Juergen) surmised that there may have been an electrical failure, and the Ram-air-turbo was being used—a fan deployed outside the aircraft to generate electricity, but it can only be used below a certain speed. We were diverted and landed safely in Amsterdam, where we took another flight home. Another event led to us catching the TGV train from Lyon to Paris. We were boarded on the flight waiting to depart, when it became apparent that there was an item of baggage on board belonging to no passenger. Juergen (along with a couple of others) insisted that we disembark. I was relieved, as due to the start of the Gulf War, the terrorist threat was very high. In any case, I welcomed the opportunity to enjoy the super-fast train ride.

For some time I was apprehensive about flying on the early Airbus aircraft, as (at that time) they seemed to have developed a nasty habit of flying into mountains—apparently, a problem with the navigation system software.

When my sister May's husband Des retired in America, he took on a consultancy in Thailand. Unhappily, he had a heart attack while playing golf, and died. May had to fly back to the US with his body in the cargo hold. Later she married an American she had known for some time. Unhappily, he too died of a heart attack. Perhaps she had a healthy sexual appetite—she once said to me,

> "Trouble with being old, you spend all night try-
> ing to do, what you used to do all night."

Some years later, she died of a rare disease—'Wegen-
ers'. I agreed to fly to the US and represent the UK family. It was an uncomfortable few days there, as her two
sons were at loggerheads over everything. They were
completely different personalities. Even as young children when I used to occasionally babysit them, they
were clearly different—one being more likeable than
the other—I spent most of the time acting as mediator.

The funeral though was impressive; the Ameri-
cans take these things seriously, providing a police escort for the cortege, and the family and friends acting
as Pall-bearers—myself one of them. Phillip, the
younger and nicer of the two brothers, was slightly
hippy-ish and in some kind of 'cult'. This completely
freaked out Chris—the older, and not so nice brother.
He was afraid that Phillip was going to give all his
share of the inheritance to the cult. Phillip also wanted
someone from the cult to sing at the funeral—freaking
Chris out even more. I also felt some slight concern
about how it might go down. The service was in what
seemed like a huge theatre with a stage. When the
singer took the stage at the end of the service, she sang
a very beautiful, soulful and moving song. Much to my
and Chris' relief. I was so moved, I made a point of
thanking her in the lobby, as we were leaving.

SRBA

When my sister Marie's husband Des, died from lung cancer—he had been a heavy smoker all his life—I drove up to Pudsey alone and spent some time with Marie as well as visiting Sylvia and Eddie. I drove Marie to the funeral parlour, as she wanted to view Des in his coffin. It is the only time I have seen a dead body. I was shocked to see how the cancer had completely decimated what had been a large, full-figured and strong man—my childhood mate.

Yasmine

Yasmine and I were more or less living together now, but all too soon cracks began to appear in the relationship—we could not seem to have a normal conversation without it degenerating into an argument.

Didn't matter how mundane or serious the conversation was, after ten minutes or so—argument. I would come home from the studio and sit in the kitchen with a drink, while she was preparing dinner. A simple conversation about my day at work—argument. A simple conversation about her day—argument. A simple conversation about absolutely anything—argument.

It got to the point where I avoided starting a conversation altogether—I would just sit there . . . schtum.

She was always taking exception to some perceived slight or other. I found myself living in a constant state of anxiety wondering when the next 'scene' would occur. One day, she was ironing a shirt for me and I (foolishly) started a discussion about the correct way to iron a shirt. I wasn't criticising her method, I was just trying to discuss the intricacies of shirt ironing as I had come to understand them, after twenty years' experience and watching a high-class butler on TV, demonstrating how 'one' should correctly iron a shirt. She completely flipped and never ironed another shirt for me. With hindsight, it was a mistake to start that particular discussion.

Once, when she was riding out to the airport with me at the crack of dawn, I remarked she was crazy to be doing this—crazy in love, I meant—a compliment. She was angry and never accompanied me again. There were many other similar scenes—too numerous to mention, and I couldn't remember what caused them anyway. I was beginning to think this was not really going to work . . .

I guess she suspected this, and accidentally-on-purpose became pregnant. She admitted later to playing Russian roulette with her contraception.

She told me she was pregnant during a business trip to Paris. I was due to meet the contractors who were German and as my German-speaking client (Juergen) could not accompany me on this trip, he arranged a ticket for Yasmine to act as my translator. We decided to make a weekend of it.

Past Tense

Rising early Friday, to catch the first flight out of LHR, Yasmine starts behaving erratically, tearfully, saying I didn't want her to come and other emotional stuff—this as I was trying to leave to get the flight. I said,

"I've arranged tickets for you and I want you, I
  need you to come. But we must leave now."
After further hesitation, she grabbed her coat.

Champagne breakfast on the flight—all was well with the world again. But then, during the meeting with the ticket office staff, Yasmine just could not resist offering an opinion while we were discussing my layout plan. She completely misread the plan, thinking a line of desks, were a wall? . . . The manageress looked at her in bewilderment and I just wanted the ground to open up and swallow me—but I quickly diverted attention and moved on with the discussion.

After Friday's business, on Saturday and Sunday, we did some nice sightseeing together—the Louvre, boat trip on the Seine. We of course had a terrible argument later, about what I cannot remember—I had not mentioned her faux pas during the meeting.

A whole afternoon and evening were wasted. I was laid on the hotel bed in despair, listening to the sound of a choir practising—the music emanating (through the open window) from an adjacent building.

Flying back to London Monday morning, speaking once more and glasses of champagne in hand, she raises the subject of our possible, future love child—

Yasmine

Manon.

"Do you still want her?"

"Yes, of course", I replied.

"Good", she said,

"Because she's well on her way."

I guess this piece of news was the reason for her erratic behaviour, over the weekend.

Later, when out with her parents in Richmond Park, she demands to know whether I will marry her or shall she have an abortion? I had grave doubts about our relationship, believing (were it not for the pregnancy) it probably could not last. But I was still besotted with her, and couldn't bear the thought of walking away. So marriage it was.

Before I married Yasmine, Kate asked me to meet her for dinner. She was talking about how she thought about me, every single day. After the meal we left, and in the car park she was shouting at me while I was trying to drive away,

"You're dumping me for a piece of twenty-six year old ass!"

I found this incredible, as it was she who had dumped me for a 'younger piece of ass'.

In the early days of our separation I would have gladly accepted her back, but despite her indicating on several occasions that she regretted the situation, she would not make the necessary declaration of intent,

"It was a mistake, I've left him, it's over. It's

just the children and me now. We're here, if you
want us, come and get us."

But she wouldn't burn her bridges like that. She was
playing the odds, keeping her options open. There was
no way I could ever have taken her back while she was
still living with him. Sometime later she said that if I
invited Beth and Trevor (mutual friends) to our wedding, she would not invite them to hers. They were
originally her friends so I agreed not to invite them.

Kingston Registry Office with Yasmine, her parents and Daniel and Lucy. Then the reception on a
Thames boat running from Hampton Court upstream
and then returning. Yasmine had arranged for some
'alternative' priest/friend to hold a second ceremony
on the boat. I hated the idea, and found it embarrassing
to say the least. But hey . . . anything to please Yasmine.
I would do almost anything to please her and didn't
ask for much in return. I couldn't understand why she
was always finding something to get upset about. We
then took Daniel and Lucy home, stopping for a meal
on the way to celebrate Lucy's Birthday, which was the
following day.

The next day we set off for our honeymoon in
Devon, spending our first night in Woody Bay. Surprisingly, the honeymoon was argument free, with lots
of delicious sex in picturesque surroundings.

When Yasmine and I married, Kate married her
lover and eventually had a son—William. When the

marriage failed, Kate went off the rails a bit, to the extent that at one point, Daniel and Lucy came to live with Yasmine and me for a short while.

Despite the divorce, Kate and I remained friends and I do still care about her, and wish it could have been different. She has been unlucky health wise and is now a shadow of her former self.

During our early courtship, Yasmine had told me distressing stories about her relationship with her parents. The stories made me terrified of meeting them—when I did eventually meet them prior to the wedding, they seemed to me (at face value) to be very pleasant. Her relationship with her brother Mike was dreadful—he refused to acknowledge her existence, and would only speak to her via a third party—usually one of the parents.

Yasmine and Mike were both born in Dhaka. Her Bangladeshi father was a barrister and her German mother worked at the German embassy there.

They then spent some years in Germany living with relatives, while their parents established themselves in London. The bad atmosphere in her family stemmed from a relationship Yasmine had with a somewhat older German cousin, while she was at University in Germany—she was only seventeen at the time.

Mike had all kinds of issues and one weekend when we were visiting him at the family home in Kingston, Yasmine asked me to take him out for a drink and see if I could talk him around to some kind of normality, regarding the family. It was not to be—he said he hated all his family and wished they were dead. I could find no sense or reason in his attitude. I couldn't get through to him. While he was always nice to me, and I found him easy to talk with, he was nevertheless a disturbed individual.

Prior to meeting me, Yasmine had been engaged to a Greek boy (Chris). She told me she had finished the relationship with him before she met me, but he refused to accept the situation. He was constantly phoning our flat, but whenever I answered, he just hung up. This made me feel angry at times—and a little threatened by his rude behaviour. Yasmine said,

"He's just a friend and in time he will accept that."
I said, "If he is a friend, he must accept me and be
my friend too."

I kept insisting she break with him, but she always refused. In time, I came to realise Yasmine would never let anyone, or anything go. They were her possessions—to be retained at all cost.

When we took Daniel on holiday with us to Spetses, it inevitably degenerated into a disaster. It was so bad one day, when we went on an organised cultural excursion and the coach stopped for lunch, Yasmine went and sat at a table with some complete strangers, rather than sit with us. They gave her some strange looks. I do not recall the reason for this.

Yasmine

This was the last straw for me and I told her that Daniel and I were going to get the next available flight home. A big emotional scene, but we stayed on. It was always like this—always wondering when the next drama would occur, and never understanding why. It was the same when we took both Daniel and Lucy to Crete. Perhaps there was something fundamentally wrong with the way I handled our relationship, but I know not what it was. I believe she felt threatened by my children, and resented the attention I gave them. It was difficult as I only saw them every week or so, and wanted to give them as much attention as possible, perhaps to the exclusion of Yasmine. I felt she should understand that. Daniel always seemed to enjoy Yasmine's company and continued visiting, even after our marriage. Conversely, Lucy seldom visited before, or after the wedding—I believe Kate discouraged her from doing so. Also Lucy had been the 'women of the house' until Yasmine's arrival on the scene.

Yasmine has a very intense, romantic view of things, whereas I am much more down-to-earth. She would sometimes say things that were straight out of some schoolgirl's romantic novel.

We were living in the top floor flat of a house in Lordship Park, which I had purchased after the breakup with Kate. When the flat on the floor below us became available, we were happy to purchase it.

I refurbished the whole flat, particularly the rear room

which opened onto a roof terrace. The plan was we could use this room and terrace while subletting the front area of the flat. This we did for two years or so, but then it remained empty and gradually became a storage area for Yasmine's possessions. Before the flat was first let, I had bought Daniel a radio-controlled truck for his birthday, and we used to play with it in the empty front room. We constructed an obstacle course filling the whole room, and competed to be the first to complete the course.

We also bought two adjacent, holiday bungalows in Greece, and we spent our summer holidays there. I didn't really want to buy them as I considered them a poor financial investment—I felt the money would be far better invested in London. However, to please Yasmine I agreed.

I could spend as much as five weeks there, taking my laptop so I could continue working and responding to client's queries. Daniel would make daily visits to the office, to deal with mail and phone messages. This arrangement worked well. We had some lovely times there, but of course there were many arguments—times spent under a cloud—in a sunny climate.

As another investment, Yasmine wanted me to buy a house further along Lordship Park. It was identical to the one we were living in. I did not like the idea as it was close to the traffic light junction with Green Lanes, but to please her, I explored the financial feasibility. It became obvious it was impossible for me to raise the necessary finance, but Yasmine did not believe that to be the case—she was desperately suggesting all kinds of crazy financial wangles, so she could obtain the property. She has never forgiven me for not buying that house.

Our second daughter Cosima had now arrived on the scene and I bought a nice retro, chrome steel cot Yasmine had admired, from the charity shop on Highbury corner—she was a frequent visitor there. I installed it in our bedroom, but it was never used. It became yet another receptacle for Yasmine's growing collection. Cosima more often than not slept in our bed.

Later Cosima was sharing Manon's bedroom, but when Manon got older we wanted her to have her own room. Manon and I suggested to Yasmine, we convert the lower flat into our living floor, with the upper flat becoming three bedrooms—the living room being the master bedroom. Yasmine wouldn't commit to the idea but agreed we should give our bedroom to Manon while Cosima would have the smaller bedroom. We would sleep downstairs. Yasmine only slept with me there, once or twice.

Yasmine's frequent scenes would often lead to her taking the girls off to her parents in Kingston, for the weekend.

232

Past Tense

She would tell the girls,

"Your father doesn't love you."

Saying this in my presence and (I am sure) frequently behind my back. I thought this was an appalling way to behave—why would a parent hurt their children like that. Even if it were true, it is still inexcusable. It seemed she was perhaps trying to turn them against me. To hurt me through them. The effect of this was demonstrated on more than one occasion—On the occasions Yasmine wasn't around, Cosima would cuddle up to me on the sofa, while we were watching TV together, then. . . Yasmine would enter the room, and Cosima to spring away from me to avoid being caught showing me affection.

In 2004, I spent the winter sleeping alone in the freezing, lower flat living room; I couldn't get to repair the central heating boiler because of Yasmine's stuff stored in the kitchen—I simply could not get into the room.

To get to the bed, I had to pick my way precariously, over mounds of plastic bin bags full of what I considered rubbish, but to Yasmine was all useful stuff.

I had a heated blanket running all night, as well as being covered in an assortment of blankets and coats. It was so depressing. Meanwhile, I could be flying to Europe two or three times a week—mostly day trips, which was tiring. Getting the first flight out of LHR and usually the last one back. These return flights were often completely booked—my free tickets (provided by BA), were always subject to commercial demand, which meant I could be bumped off the flight by any fare-paying passenger who wanted the last seat. This never actually happened because the flight staff would always apologise and say,

"Mr Burnett, would you mind terribly, sitting in the cockpit jump-seat?"

I would reply,

"Oh dear, never mind, that will be okay."

I absolutely loved it when this happened—the cockpit jump-seat is the best seat on any aircraft. The seat pivots out and locates centrally, between the Captain and Co-Pilot, but at a slightly higher level. This allows you to look directly out of the cockpit windows—an even better view than the pilots. Taking off and landing was always breath taking. I particularly loved coming into London after dark—depending on the wind direction, the approach path would usually be along the Thames, and over the city centre.

Flights to Rome, Milan, Barcelona and Madrid, would always involve overnight stays. Much less tiring and far more enjoyable as I was able to see the city, have a nice dinner and stay in a swanky hotel. Rome and Barcelona were my favourites.

When BA re-launched the 'Club Europe' product, I redesigned the seven main European lounges. This involved much travelling around Europe to check progress with the local clients, consultants and contractors. The 'flagship lounge' for the re-launch was in Charles de Gaulle Airport, Paris. Due to lack of space it was located in old storage areas in the Basement below Satellite-5, apron level. This required the installation of access lifts from the departures gate as well as special features and lighting, to create a sense of natural daylight.

All seven lounges opened on the same day, so it was decided I would be at Charles de Gaulle Airport lounge for the final snagging and official opening. The night before, my client Juergen and the BA local airport manageress had a lovely dinner together, and then we were given a tour of a Concorde that was waiting to be boarded for a charter flight. Afterwards, we went down and stood on the apron drinking champagne in the dark, while watching Concorde take off into the night sky. It does not get much better. Everything was going fine . . . then—9/11.

I had 13 projects on my desk, including a massive new project at LHR Terminal 1. That Tuesday morning I was driving back to London from a meeting at BA headquarters, when I got a call on my mobile from one of the people who had attended the meeting. He told me about the Trade Centre attack and said,

"I'll be looking for a job by the end of the week."
He was right.
Every one of my 13 projects was immediately frozen

and hundreds of people at BA were made redundant. Suddenly, I had absolutely no work. Fortunately for me the LHR, Terminal 1 project was too big and (as the Airport Authority had already started construction of a new building to house this project) too expensive to stop—the penalty fees would be more than the cost of continuing. Therefore, after considering the financial implications of cancelling the project, three months later in the New Year it was restarted. It was a massive project for me—the biggest ever. This was two years of really hard, interesting (and sometimes exciting) slog. Daniel was a big help during this period.

6:05 24th October 2003—the last flight of Concorde. What an emotional day that was. Having designed its second interior scheme (I think it had four over its life-time) I felt particularly connected to it. It was such a beautiful machine—fantastic example of form follow-ing function. Of course the interior was quite cramped—it was good that passengers got where they were going quickly. It was also incredibly noisy. Whenever I was at BA headquarters for meetings, come twelve noon we would have to halt the proceed-ings, while Concorde took off and roared overhead.

On the day, I was down at LHR attending site meetings, and I went into one of the lounges with a couple of BA clients. From there we had a grandstand view of the three Concorde landing and parking in front of the lounge windows. There were women crying everywhere — and I think, some men. I too felt emotional. We had a few drinks and I was glad to have been there. It was sad to see such a step into the future disappear — I feel the same way about the moon landings. Such an achievement and now nothing. From a boots-on-the-ground point of view anyway.

When the Shoreditch Studio lease ended, I rented an office in a Camden Town, business centre for a few years. Then, in 2004, the Lordship garden flat came up for sale and we bought it, initially to use as my office, but also as an investment. The rear, two garden rooms became my office, and the rest of the flat I gradually renovated. Four months later, the one remaining upper, ground floor flat came up for sale, and it seemed to make sense to buy it and own the whole house. We were supposed to sublet it, but instead it quickly filled with Yasmine's possessions. She was constantly buying furniture and other items at auction houses — she would often call me and ask me to collect (and pay for) some item she'd purchased from an auction house. None of this stuff was needed and I certainly didn't want it. But whenever I complained she would say,

"I can't help it, I'm a collector."

Her other justification for buying things was she could sell them at a profit. Of course — she never did sell anything. It became clear to me and the children, she was not a collector; she was 'a hoarder.'

237

Yasmine

Hoarding is an illness and it gradually became worse. Every spare inch of space, in every room became filled with her 'stuff.' One flat was completely full—you could not enter any of the rooms. Hoarders are often indecisive and this was certainly true of Yasmine. It is said there is a link between a previous family member being a hoarder and having the disorder yourself. Yasmine's mother also hoarded old newspapers and other items, and was even more indecisive than Yasmine. Past trauma can also be a root cause of hoarding—on two occasions while she was a young child living in Bangladesh, the family lost their home, and all their possessions. First to a typhoon, then again when the 1971 Liberation war erupted and they had to abandon everything. Her parents knew they had to flee the country, along with several million others. The day before they were all to fly out of the country—on the last flight—Yasmine (against strict instructions) played with a stray dog, and was bitten. Her parents went crazy and beat her. In a panic, they had to organise a tetanus injection for her, before catching the flight.

With this and other issues, I feel the parents are responsible for both Mike's and Yasmine's personality issues.

The Empress State Building and Earls Court Exhibition Hall London. During my early years in London, I lived at various locations around and close to this build-

238

ing—bed-sitter-land! While living in Philbeach Gardens, or 'Kangaroo Alley' as it was called locally (and where I encountered the lady who gifted me gonorrhoea), people would queue past our front door to see the 'Motor Show' at Earls Court. Had some great times and some not so great there. Lots of parties with dreadful, cheap, Spanish wine. Consequently I was put off Spanish wine for years until I spent some time in Barcelona, on a project there for British Airways. The local client introduced me to Rioja and it's been one of my favourite red wines ever since.

During my days as an exhibition designer, I would often spend whole days (and nights) in the exhibition halls, supervising the installation of exhibits for various clients. So it felt strange (years later) to be asked by the Metropolitan Police to assist them with their planned move of the 'Fingerprint' department into the building. Even stranger, my first wife Kate and our daughter Lucy were by this time both working for the Metropolitan Police. I did not see that coming. The Empress State Building—thirty-one floors high and most floors holding about 150 people. This was a lot of people and a lot of desks, filing cabinets etc. The Met had taken over the whole building as part of their property portfolio rationalisation.

For me it was simply a space planning exercise, with little creative design. However, it was a large project and this made it interesting and more importantly, lucrative. Daniel was still working with me, and was a great help—I could not have managed otherwise. This project arrived at just the right time, as (with the end of the LHR Terminal 1 project) work was a bit thin on the ground.

The project completion was on Guy Fawkes night and Yasmine and I were invited to celebrate the occasion in the top (31ˢᵗ) floor, rotating bar. A great view and an interesting evening, with fireworks (from the surrounding houses) going off literally around our ears.

One Christmas, Yasmine got into a rage about something and locked herself in the lower-flat, rear room for the whole period. Manon and I talked and I told her this could not go on much longer. She was fully aware of the situation and of course, upset. This Christmas episode was the last straw for me and I left Yasmine in August 2005, moving into the garden flat. She and the girls were in our holiday home in Greece at the time—I thought it would be less upsetting for the girls this way, but Yasmine and her parents considered me a coward.

Friday nights the girls would come down for dinner, and after we would watch a film together. I enjoyed these evenings a great deal. While I was preparing dinner, the girls would be dancing around the living room—they couldn't do this upstairs because there was no room to dance. Cosima also had dinner with me on Wednesday evenings, while Manon and Yasmine went to an adult dancing class.

Cosima was passionate about dance and was very skilful. She attended various dance classes and competed successfully in competitions. One was in Barcelona and Yasmine accompanied her there. Unsurprisingly, Yasmine managed to miss the return flight.

Cosima had to be back in London for an operation at Great Ormond Street hospital the next day, so to make sure she was back in time, I had to pay £500 for another ticket. This was typical of Yasmine's chaotic life routine—everything was always difficult, complicated, convoluted and late. I am sad that due to the lack of money we were unable to encourage Cosima's dancing skills further. A close childhood friend of Cosima went on to the 'Italia Conti' School. He was not as good a dancer as Cosima, but his parents were able to pay the substantial fees required. Cosima also has a passion for acting and is now studying Drama at Goldsmiths University.

Yasmine took the separation badly. Through some crazy, illogical reasoning she blamed Manon, saying she encouraged me to leave—saying she could have prevented it. Manon gradually became weary of the constant, screaming arguments with Yasmine and asked if she could come and live with me in flat A. I of course agreed. She was sleeping on the sofa bed and I made space for her in one of the rear rooms, where she could keep all her belongings and use it as a dressing room. When—due to ongoing back problems—I finally had to stop playing my beloved Squash. Eric, my friend and regular squash opponent used to play pool with me after his squash session, so we then started playing snooker together. We were playing at a small club in Camden Town where the manager and his wife were friendly to us. One evening while they were not there, a plumber arrived to fix the blocked toilets.

The person behind the desk didn't think to tell anyone about this and the plumber had not placed any warning barrier. It was always dark around the toilets and in I walk to take a pee—and fall straight down into the open manhole, up to my thighs in urine and excrement.

Apart from the disgusting circumstances, it was also painful. After I had recovered from the shock and as we were leaving, the person behind the desk asked us to pay for the table. We did not pay and never went back again. The club was due to close anyway, due to planned redevelopment.

I had met Rodney again at the club—we had originally joined the club together years earlier, before I stopped playing. Rodney, Eric and I played a few frames together on a couple of occasions. Sadly, soon after meeting up again, I received a phone call from Leonard Hutton telling me that Rodney had died, and inviting me to the funeral. The ceremony was very moving and most of the 'clan' and other friends were present. The chapel had large, full height windows all around, and towards the end of the ceremony there was suddenly large crashes of thunder and lightning—very dramatic—I'm sure Rodney would have approved. It was nice seeing so many old friends, and we all went to the wake in a nearby pub. I was sorry to have lost contact with Rodney—I guess it was a result of two failed marriages and a great deal of work pressure—but no excuse, really.

I fell into conversation with John Dover, who I hadn't seen since the unhappy holiday we spent together in Ramatuelle, with Kate and Wendy. He mentioned Kate and said,

"Oh, you got a right one there."

I thought cheeky bastard, and walked away from him—this is the guy who screwed Wendy's best friend—while she was in the hospital having his baby. That incident had hung like a black cloud over the holiday.

While Marie had been nursing Des with help of a charity nurse, the nurse became aware Marie was bleeding from a nipple. Yes it was cancer, but being caught and treated so soon, she lived for some years after. Eventually, she succumbed to Alzheimer's and other issues. My sister Sylvia had a difficult time looking after Marie towards the end, and dealing with her affairs after her death. I drove up to attend the funeral with Lucy, my grandson Sydney, Daniel and Cosima. Despite the sad occasion, it was nice for them to meet (for the first time as adults) with Sylvia and her family. We spent a pleasant few hours at my niece Michele's house. We then drove back to Bradford and had dinner in our hotel there. Cosima had her favourite—roast chicken and gravy. I was touched the three kids had volunteered to accompany me to the funeral, without any prompting on my part. Manon was at university in Germany at the time, and could not attend. Sadly, Manon has not met any of the northern branch of my family—living or dead.

The American, sub-prime financial crisis arrived in 2008, and that was the end of my business. I was working solely on British Airways projects at that time, and they just stopped every project I was working on. This was worse than 9/11. No quick recovery this time. I quickly began to run out of money. I was making payments on four mortgages, four electricity bills, four gas bills, four water rates, four council tax bills and my credit cards were all maxed out.

Despite my many attempts to persuade her to do so, Yasmine refused to sell any of her possessions or any of the four flats. Eventually, I had no choice but to start divorce proceedings. We were living off money borrowed from her family and—to a greater extent—my first family. My good friend Eric also kindly loaned me £1,000, so that the girls could go to Greece for the summer holiday. Yasmine's parents were always reluctant to lend money. For a long time, they shunned Yasmine and also Manon and Cosima. They were afraid that if Yasmine visited, she would ask for more money, or bring stuff to store, or both. So they would not allow any of the family to visit their home in Kingston Vale. This was a stressful time, for everyone.

My solicitor confirmed my belief that it was a clear case for a 50/50 split of all the assets. But of course Yasmine refused to accept this, claiming she should have more. She would not agree to any offer around the 50% mark, so we had to go to trial.

The result was (on the 12th November 2012), the Judge confirmed it should indeed be a 50/50 split. Yasmine appealed against the judgement and failed. This resulted in joint legal fees of around £200k. We were both £100k poorer, simply because she refused to be rational, reasonable, or just plain fair.

We have not spoken since, and probably never will— apparently she regards me as the devil incarnate.

Present Tense

There is so much more I could say about my two failed marriages—the nitty-gritty of the relationships, what was said, what was done, and when, by whom to whom, but I am restrained by the wish to avoid offence, mainly to my children, but also my two ex-wives. I have also avoided going into too much detail about the various women I had the pleasure to encounter throughout my life. That would have been ungentlemanly and would have embarrassed the hell out of my children—the girls anyway.

Were Kate and Yasmine to write their versions of this book, I'm sure it would be very different. I've tried to think what I could have done to make things work in the two marriages, but I am at a loss—I was faithful and never asked for much, other than a peaceful life, with plenty of love and affection. I was not cruel and did not physically abuse them. Okay, I certainly worked too hard, but you have no choice when running your own business, you cannot say no to clients—they may never ask again. I guess men are generally not very good at understanding women, or being aware of what it is they should be doing to make things better.

Two years after I had separated from Yasmine (while I was still living in flat A), I began to feel lonely, especially as I was then less preoccupied with work. I decided to try online dating. I subsequently met some nice women and had some pleasant times, but it could be frustrating. There is so much dishonesty on dating sites. The photographs women post can be anything up to twenty years out of date and they always, always lie about their age—usually deleting ten years or more. They would often confess this on the first date, claiming it was standard practice. I could not understand how they could expect to start a relationship, with a lie.

Though I had several unsuccessful dates, I always figured it was usually better to spend an evening talking to a (hopefully nice) lady, than staying in alone—scratching my bum. Having said that, some dates were dreadful—seeing her approaching across the bar or restaurant, and wishing the ground would open up and swallow me. I would be waiting full of anticipation for the woman in the photographs, hoping I would recognise her—and her mother would turn up. If you were unlucky, her grandmother.

Present Tense

I never did escape through the rear emergency exit, but a couple of dates told me, they had done just that. Initially, I usually felt committed to having a meal with them, but after a while, I toughened up and only committed to a glass of wine or coffee, before excusing myself.

I met one woman in a pub off High Street Kensington. I arrived early evening (as usual ahead of the arranged time), the bar was quiet and I slipped into the routine—bought a glass of wine (Dutch courage), checked out the surroundings, chose the best seat with a good view of the entrance and where she could easily see me. If I was particularly nervous, I allowed time to drink one glass of wine, and have another just started, ready for the moment of truth. Eventually, she arrived—late. She began jabbering nervously and I went to the bar to buy her wine. In response to considerable noise, coming from her direction, the barman said to me,

"What is she doing?"

I turned to see she was re-arranging the tables and chairs . . .

"Don't ask me," I said, and returned to the table's new location, with her drink. After her nervous chatter about her domestic arrangements and why she was late, I decided it was time to go. I finished my wine and took my leave, as graciously as possible. She was disappointed, expecting to make an evening of it. Meeting another lady in St Johns bar, Smithfield Market one evening (our second date), I was (due to rush hour traffic) a little late. I rushed in and pulled a chair around the table, to be seated closer to her. After returning from the bar with a drink, I was astounded to realise that I was sitting opposite, and almost within touching distance of Kristin Scott-Thomas—one of my all time, favourite female, actresses. She was sitting with her daughter on the adjacent table.

I'm proud to say I handled myself well, not a moments pause of attention to my date, and I didn't spill my drink. But my pulse was surely faster.

I can honestly say, I noticed her clocking me a couple of times—*YES!*

Another woman messaged me on the dating site and became indignant when I didn't respond immediately. Her profile contained only a portrait photo. She had an attractive face with blue eyes and silky, blond hair. Off I drove all the way down to her home in Rye.

No sooner had I arrived and sat down, she straddled me and planted a wide-open kiss on my face—I mean, all my face. I thought she was going to swallow my head. I love kissing—but not empty space. I managed to fend her off and we left for the lunch reservation she had arranged.

After lunch, we made our way back to her place, where she continued her onslaught. I removed my watch (because the clasp kept coming undone) and she said,

"Well, that's one thing off."

I thought "Oh, oh!"

She clearly was expecting to have sex. I was aghast. Taking a deep breath, I said,

"I'm sorry, but I don't want to go any further with this, and I'm going to leave now."

On the doorstep, she was tearful and said,

"But this is like a second date."

What? I didn't understand how she arrived at that conclusion—if she had possessed even the most rudimentary skill in the art of kissing, it might (possibly) have been different.

I had two minor relationships and one serious, that lasted a couple of years, until she finished it. It was the third time she had finished it, but this time she didn't change her mind. She lived in Norfolk and we were only together at weekends. She wanted me to make a big commitment, but given I was (at that time) in the middle of a difficult divorce, I was unwilling to make the situation more complicated than it already was. She also expected me to solve her financial difficulties, which I was in no position to do. It's a pity because she was very nice; we had a great deal in common, and got on very well.

One woman had a fabulous 'Huf' house on a hillside outside London. I visited her twice, spending the weekend with her on the second visit. My flat had an alarm system I had installed, that would call my mobile or the flat D landline if there was a problem—burglary or fire. Because I didn't want to be disturbed that weekend, I turned my mobile off. Unfortunately, in the middle of the night, a problem developed with the alarm—the system kept trying to dial, first me and then flat D.

Cosima kept answering the phone (Yasmine would never do so), only to hear my recorded voice saying,

"Burglar, burglar, burglar!"

Yasmine called the police out, but they could not help. Cosima told me that afterwards, Yasmine was running around with a frying pan in her hand. Poor Manon, who was spending the night at her boyfriends, returned to provide help and support. Eventually, the system shut down—I sure got a lot of flak on my return. I could not find any problem with the system—I think perhaps a spider had got into a sensor—consequently, I was too nervous to activate the alarm again. Fortunately, I did not remain in the property much longer.

Eventually, as stipulated in the divorce agreement, the properties were sold and I was able to buy my current Hornsey flat in September 2013. The building society messed up the paperwork and I had to find somewhere to live for a week—Kate kindly allowed me to stay with her until the money came through. All my furniture and possessions had to be put in storage for the week.

Present Tense

As Manon had already chosen to live with me in the Lordship flat, she moved here with me. She was now able to have her own bedroom. Time has passed, and she is now living and working in southern Germany, where she has her own flat. She is as happy as she can be, that is until she finds the right man to raise a family with. She did German literature at Kings College, but I don't think she is a career woman—she really wants to have a family.

Cosima also lived here with Manon and me for a few months. It was impossible for her to live with Yasmine, in the chaotic and cluttered living spaces. She also enjoyed being with Manon—they have always been exceptionally close. Yasmine retained flat C in the divorce settlement and is now living there. She had also acquired flat D (as a buy to let) through some strange deal with some weird guy. I met him when (at Yasmine's prompting) he came to try to buy the garden flat. I didn't like him at all and gave him short thrift. After some time when one of the tenants living in flat D left, at Yasmine's invitation, Cosima was able to move back into her old bedroom. This also allowed her to be close to her mum and provide emotional support. She still cares a great deal her mum.

Cosima visits me a couple of times a week. She is at Goldsmiths University doing 'Theatre Studies'. We have dinner and watch a film together. Manon visits us from Germany when she can, but Cosima and I both miss her a great deal.

My eldest daughter Lucy has always worked very hard in whatever job she had. She is now a 'Detective Sargent' with the Metropolitan police, and I am sure she will progress much higher in the ranks—although she doesn't want to end up in a desk job. She wants to remain 'hands on'. With her partner Steve, she also has a son—Sydney—my first grandchild. He is a very sweet child, handsome and bright as a button.

Daniel having worked with me on and off, for two or three years, I thought perhaps he might follow in my footsteps in some way. But design was not for him. He was always good with computers and is now doing well as an IT consultant for a travel organisation. He recently married Anna—a lovely girl, and he seems very happy. I hope he (and anyone else who reads this book) finds it interesting—I will be content if I can at least, persuade the children, to read it—this is not a given . . .

Since I moved here, I have been keeping a low profile and have not bothered with online dating until just recently, when (without success) I went on a couple of dates. I took up Archery while I was still in Lordship Park and became quite good at a club level, until I injured my back a couple of years ago. I have been unable to practice archery since then, until recently. Time will tell whether I can get back into it. Various medical issues also impacted on my health and involved a couple of stays in hospital. Finally, after the removal of my gall-bladder, I am trying very hard to build up my strength and overall general fitness again—I'm going to the gym regularly and getting stronger. But the break seems to have quenched my passion for the sport—I was a bit obsessed with it. It's always like that with me—it was the same with squash, playing every day and even twice a day sometimes. Recurring injuries put paid to that. I used to think I would be unable to exist without playing squash, but once the spell is broken . . .

So now I am kind of suffering from a double whammy—being retired and suffering from the 'Empty Nester' syndrome.

My brother Eddie was the next to die—he had been ill for some time. Lucy and I travelled up by train and returned the same day. After the funeral, on the way back to the station, we had a pleasant lunch with Sylvia and her husband, Melvyn.

My unhappy thought is the next and final time I visit the North, will be for Sylvia's funeral—assuming I don't die first. She is nine years older than me.

Maybe I will be invited to Melvyn's funeral—probably, if he dies before Sylvia.

Then, it will be my turn.

Present Tense

Through work, I had some fun times and got to travel around the world a lot more than I might otherwise have done. Although I was never a 'big name' designer, I was lucky enough to be involved in a lot of quality work, for major international clients.

So now, it looks like I'm retired. It's not something I've ever really thought about, I've always been far too busy working - usually 24/7.

What to do?

I understand some people spend their working lives planning and looking forward to retirement, preferably an early one, so they can take to the golf course. It has never been like that for me and, like (I imagine) most creative people, I always assumed I would go on doing what I enjoy until the day I die.

Time moves on and you adapt as best you can. Some days I actually quite like being retired—though I do get restless at times—restless, bored and lonely. It has given me the time to write this book, but whether this is a good or bad thing, remains to be seen. Sometimes when I run out of things to do or just can't summon up the energy to do them, I get very bored—and depressed. It's difficult to remain positive and energetic, filling the days with interesting activities. There are various hobbies, activities I have identified, but finding the enthusiasm and energy to make a start on one of them—is often beyond me. That said there's no way I would like to go back to the relentless pressure of deadline driven design work. While I was still shooting archery regularly and was a committee member with Hampstead Bowmen, I was very involved with various aspects of the club relating to the outdoor shooting range. That often kept me occupied, but my back injury stopped that. I also fell foul of amateur, club committee politics, and that influenced my enjoyment of the club social activities. I have also undertaken various small design projects for others and myself. The latest project being for a local group—'Friends of Alexandra Park'. My local park that I have fond memories of, when Kate and I lived close by. I would be a frequent visitor with the children at weekends.

On one of my recent walks, I visited an area of the park that brought back the memory of Daniel and me trying to fly a kite there. It was a kite based on the Vickers-Rolls-Royce symbol designed while at Negus & Negus. It was a windy day, and it immediately got stuck in a large tree—that was the end of that.

I remember taking Lucy to the playground there one Sunday. There was an accident on the swings and she banged her head badly. I had to carry her, walking and running as fast as I could, all the way home. I then drove her and Kate to the Whittington—she survived.

How I hate growing old. Over the last forty years or so, I have usually been fairly fit and active —trained for the very first London marathon, cycled to work every day, played squash (every day at first) until my back complained too much —my back doesn't like the archery a lot either. One positive result of a couple of recent visits to the hospital is that I have managed to lose a significant amount of weight. People keep telling me I don't look seventy-six, perhaps I don't. I am sometimes shocked when I encounter what I consider to be an old man, only to discover that he is my age— or even younger. This could be (on more than one occasion), quite embarrassing—in a social gathering or worse still—a business meeting with clients. There would often be some annoying character, who would raise the question of age,

"And how old are you Stewart?"

What was really cringe making, was when he would ask someone, perhaps a restaurant waitress (as she came to take our order),

"Who do you think is the oldest person among
Us three?"

Arrrrgh.

So yes, I have difficulty with the concept of being old— I am not old . . . I cannot be . . .

But I am (of course) old. More and more, I find myself being shocked to catch a glimpse of my body in the bathroom mirror and notice yet another dreaded sign of age—varicose veins, wrinkles to the upper arms, and others I prefer not to mention here.

Women joke about men who think they are a twenty-five-year-old located in an old man's body—but it is actually like that. In my mind, I do not feel old, and I feel frustrated by the realisation that I can't actually carry out certain physical activities. I no longer relish the thought of some little DIY project. I think I just need to keep going to the gym, and that does help, but there are limits that my age alone prevents me from exceeding—I am not referring to sex, I hasten to add— after seven years abstinence, that remains to be seen . . .

What is a failed marriage? Whatever it is, I've had two of 'em. Apparently, over 40% of marriages fail—or simply just end. According to the Office for National Statistics, on average a marriage lasts about eleven years. I think Kate must have checked the ONS figures because that's exactly how long our marriage lasted. The second marriage beat the odds and lasted sixteen years.

I do recall the overwhelming sense of failure when the first marriage to Kate ended. It was as if I had suddenly become a rejected member of society, to be shunned by all around me. Everyone else was carrying on, living (what seemed to me) their successful, happy lives. Whereas I did not belong anymore—a leper, an outcast. Why had this happened to me? I could not believe I deserved it.

Apart from these imagined consequences, there were actual rejections. Mutual friends sometimes take sides, voluntarily, or under pressure from one side other the other. I remember two good friends of ours being told by Kate that, if they were to attend my marriage to Yasmine, they would not be invited to attend hers—to the man she had replaced me with.

There were two children from each marriage, and inevitably, there is a great deal of guilt involved regarding them, and concern for their future wellbeing. Because of the divorce, they have all suffered, and I have always felt guilty for my part in it—they have all missed opportunities they might otherwise have benefitted from.

However, all four have grown to become beautiful, intelligent, well-spoken and decent people. So were the marriages failures? If the purpose of marriage is to bear children, then perhaps not.

I was never the 'Earth Father'—I was not desperate to have children. Getting married and raising a family, was never my raison-d'etre; but I have always enjoyed and loved my children—I still do.

It's amazing how different they can be—the only consistent thing about them is they are all tall and beautiful—they get this from me of course . . .

I worry that perhaps I'm becoming a bit reclusive— with hermit tendencies. I often feel lonely and yearn for adult and especially female companionship. Then I think, oh gawd, it's all too much trouble—and anyway, it usually ends in tears.

However, I'm sure that if I met the right woman, I would wholeheartedly go for it—but then again . . . maybe not.

I used to find all this confusing . . . but now, I'm not so sure.

I came across the following online and found it amusing and (in my case), prophetic:

A man will pay £2 for a £1 item that he needs—while a woman, will pay £1 for a £2 item, she does not need. And she will continue doing so . . .

To be happy with a man, a woman must understand him a lot, and love him a little.

To be happy with a woman, a man must love her a lot, and not try to understand her at all.

There are two times when a man does not understand a woman—before marriage, and after marriage.

A woman marries a man believing she can change him, but usually, she cannot—while a man marries a woman praying that she will never change, but of course, she does.

Present Tense

A woman has the last word in any argument—anything a man says after that is the beginning of a new argument.

Any married man should forget his mistakes—there is no use in two people remembering the same, annoying, things.

And boy . . . they sure remember everything.

Printed in Great Britain
by Amazon